GOLF
ETIQUETTE 101

GOLF ETIQUETTE 101

Your Guide to Proper Behavior on the Course and in the Clubhouse

BILL BAILEY

PRIMA PUBLISHING

PRIMA PUBLISHING and colophon are registered trademarks of Prima Communications, Inc.

Previously published under the title *Protocol and Etiquette of Golf* by Prima Publishing, 1994.

Library of Congress Cataloging-in-Publication Data

Bailey, Bill.
    Golf etiquette 101 : your guide to proper behavior on the course and in the clubhouse / Bill Bailey
        p.   cm.
    Rev. ed. of: Executive golf. c1985
    Includes index.
    ISBN 0-7615-1286-1
    1. Golf—Social aspects. 2. Golfers—Conduct of life. I. Bailey, Bill, Executive golf. II. Title.
GV979.S63B35 1997
796.352—dc21   97-49305
                                                                                    CIP

98 99 00 01 HH 10 9 8 7 6 5 4 3 2 1
Printed in the United States of America

How to Order
Single copies may be ordered from Prima Publishing, P.O. Box 1260BK, Rocklin, CA 95677; telephone (916) 632-4400. Quantity discounts are also available. On your letterhead, include information concerning the intended use of the books and the number of books you wish to purchase.

Visit us online at www.primapublishing.com

Bobby Jones once wrote . . .

"Golf may be . . . a sophisticated game.
At least, it is usually played with the out-
ward appearance of great dignity. It is,
nevertheless, a game of considerable
passion, either of the explosive type,
or that which burns inwardly and sears
the soul."

"There we
all were.
Strictly tux,
black tie.
And me in
my *brown* shoes."

Contents

Foreword
by Gene Littler

Bill Bailey has come home. He's at home and at ease on the golf course—any golf course. Where there could be tension, he has brought humor and relaxation. As he's added to the pleasure of his game and mine, he's made it an enjoyable "walk in the woods" for all the golfers who have joined him.

Etiquette is what Bill's book is all about. Every social and business occasion has its do's and don'ts. In golf, perhaps more than any other sport, etiquette is not just nice, it's the *only* way.

There's a proud history, a noble past, that shapes the way we play the game. In golf, honesty and good manners go hand in hand.

Golf behavior is an important subject that Bill makes into fun reading. Fun is the key. Not just to your game, but to those in the game around you.

I know Bill's purpose in writing this book is to acquaint beginning golfers with some of the tribal rituals of golf while giving old hands a little refresher course. We all need to be reminded of the heritage and traditions of golf.

I hope you enjoy Bill's book as much as I've enjoyed his splendid company on the course.

Former U.S. Open Champion and multimillion dollar winner of hundreds of professional tournaments, Gene Littler is referred to internationally as "Gene the Machine" for his flawless golf swing. His perfect golf manners may have also given a boost to his "spare time" business, a lucrative sideline, antique cars.

Preface

"It ain't how *well* you play, it's *how* you play the game!" The way you look and act says whether you're the executive type, irrespective of how high you score. The way you go about your game is one hundred times more important than how well you play. That's what *Golf Etiquette 101* is all about. We spell out proper behavior. What to wear, where to stand, when to hit, who pays, what to say—thousands of answers that can clear your way to making the best possible impression on the golf course. Big deals and promotions are often determined on the golf course, simply because golf is a favorite pastime of business leaders. A round of golf can be the most important sales "field trip" you'll ever take. Nowhere are executive skills more apparent—or more obviously lacking—than on the golf course.

Just as automobile companies have their proving grounds, big business has its proving grounds. The golf course is the *executive proving ground.*

The ironic fact of the matter is that until this guide, information on proper behavior has been so hush-hush, that at its very best, it's pretty much been "hand-me-down" vocal instructions from old-timers.

Etiquette is casually and briefly addressed in the rules of golf, which point out certain golf commandments like, "There shall be silence when another player is hitting." But the rules do not go about the task, nor should they, of determining just how your behavior can and will be translated into assets or liabilities as they affect you, the individual.

The rules are to be found in another book. How to play like a pro, in yet hundreds of other books.

Here we will examine how to look and act like a winner. We will deal with your image. And right here, let's get this word *image* pinned down. Let's sum it up by saying it's the *net impression.* Though all the details of a person may be totally forgotten, it's the sense of feeling what a person is all about. Whether we like it or not, the net impression we create becomes reality. Our image is the mortar that holds together our foundation for fun, achievement, and success.

It's quite true that as the old saying goes, "You can tell the character of a man by his behavior on the golf course." We believe some of the 23 million regular golfers will agree, you among them, because you are taking the time to read and learn about the self-image potential that golf holds for you.

All of us are in a constant state of trying to improve our image, and opportunities abound on the golf course. Once considered a sport just for the rich, the 71 percent increase in play in the past ten years is good testimony that it has spread beyond the rich, though it remains the signature sport for many of America's business people.

By choice, or by luck of the draw, it's most likely that you often will be joined up in a foursome of these business folks. And after all, people get to know you far better in a four-hour round of golf than in a brief office interview.

—Bill Bailey

Dollars and Sense
by Bruce Devlin

To Bill Bailey:

I have reviewed your book on the etiquette of golf thoroughly and believe you will be interested in these three observations:

1. If every player were to observe your pointers they would make the game immensely more enjoyable for themselves.
2. They certainly would improve their image with other golfers.
3. But now the pay-off benefits to the club course they are playing: If your pointers were followed, an average club in the Sunbelt would, in just the first year, realize a minimum savings in excess of $20,000 on golf course maintenance.

In the colder climates—shorter season—the maintenance reduction would still amount to at least $15,000 per year. Amounts like this could go a long way toward improving course aesthetics and developing a putting green, a practice range, a learning and training center, etc.

I'll be happy to substantiate these figures for any interested party.

Best of luck,

Bruce Devlin

During the past twenty-six years, Bruce Devlin has been in-volved in the design and building of 100 golf courses in many countries throughout the world, including Australia, Japan, Puerto Rico, the Bahamas, and the United States. A recent design was recognized as a Grand Triumph. It was the final design on Sessation Golf Club on Gibbes Island near Beaufort, South Carolina, which is among the few golf properties ranked as Trophy class. The founders had this to say about Devlin: "It is too seldom we have the pleasure of working with someone of your experience and dedication. We believe that Sessation will enhance your already established stature as a golf course designer."

Devlin's well rounded golf career includes six years on NBC as a golf color analyst and three years on ESPN as a Senior Tour Commentator. He has had eight major tour victories on the PGA tour, joined the Senior tour in 1987, and has won a number of championships throughout Australia.

Introduction

Some History of Golf

From the very beginning, even in its early Scottish days, golf was always a game of accuracy. The purpose of the modern game is obviously to get the small, hard ball into a $4\frac{1}{4}$ inch diameter hole in the ground in the fewest possible strokes from the time the ball has been played from the teeing area.

There are chunks of time and events omitted in the long history of golf that make speculation about its roots quite variable. We do know that it is one of the oldest of modern sports and that Scotland is credited by all authorities with devising, sometime in the fourteenth or fifteenth century, the game as we know it today.

We know for a fact the first known organized golf club was founded in 1744 by the Honourable Company of Edinburgh Golfers.

Ten years after the Honourable Company was formed, along came the Saint Andrews Society of Golfers. This organization is now known as the Royal and Ancient Golf Club of Saint Andrews. It has existed since 1754 and has become the mecca of golf.

As best we can tell, golf was played in the United States before 1888, but it was not until that year that the Saint Andrew's Golf Club of Yonkers, the first permanent American golf club, was organized.

Why any sport so capable of frustrating and humiliating the player can flourish to encompass more than 20 million players in the United States alone is a point of great conjecture.

But, as no one can deny, golf is on a roll—a roll of unheralded popularity and growth.

New golf courses are bursting through nature to accommodate millions of golfers, and the sport's popularity shows no sign of diminishing.

The United States Golf Association:
The Guardian of the Game

The USGA Rules of Golf provided the inspiration for this book. The author encourages all golfers to utilize the many helpful suggestions that are contained therein.

Let's take a moment to explain just what the USGA is all about.

Over a century ago, in 1894, a dispute arose over the question of who was the national amateur golf champion. Two different golf clubs—St. Andrew's Golf Club, in Yonkers, New York, and the Newport (R.I.) Golf Club—staged invitational competitions and declared their winner as the national amateur champion.

This rivalry and its ensuing confusion highlighted the need for an impartial governing body in the United States to administer the game, conduct national championships, and oversee the codification and interpretation of the Rules of Golf and the Rules of Amateur Status. Thus, the United States Golf Association was founded to fulfill these roles.

Dedicated to promoting the best interests of golf, the USGA today is guided by its sixteen member Executive Committee. This committee is the organization's policy-making board and represents more than 8,000 member clubs and courses and more than 350,000 individual members. Several other committees, comprised of approximately 1,000 men and women volunteers, augment the Executive Committee. The USGA also maintains a paid staff at its headquarters, Golf House, in Far Hills, New Jersey, and at several regional offices throughout the country, to conduct its affairs on a day-to-day basis.

The USGA held three national championships in 1895—the U.S. Open, the U.S. Amateur, and the Women's Amateur. The USGA's schedule now encompasses thirteen national and several international competitions.

The USGA selects the U.S. team that competes for the Walker Cup, a biennial competition between teams of amateur golfers from the United States on one side and Great Britain and Ireland on the other. Similarly, the USGA chooses members for the Curtis Cup Match, played between teams of women amateur golfers from the same nations. The USGA conducts both championships when they are played in this country.

The USGA is also active in the World Amateur Golf Council, which has conducted the World Amateur Team Championship since 1958, and the Women's World Amateur Team Championship since 1964.

Although its competition schedule represents a major portion of the USGA's annual calendar, it's only a part of the USGA's total contribution to golf. The USGA strives to maintain the integrity and values of the game by updating its Rules, formulating the handicap and golf course rating systems, regulating the Rules of Amateur Status and Conduct, testing new balls and equipment, researching turfgrasses, studying golf's impact on the environment, funding junior golf programs, and preserving golf's history through its museum at Golf House.

Although a good deal has changed about the USGA during the past century, one thing remains constant. Golf's national governing body remains dedicated to preserving, protecting, and promoting the best interests and true spirit of the game as embodied in its ancient and honorable traditions.

A Warning Bell

The sanctity of golf is being threatened. If you believe that phrase is sanctimoniously overstated, let me explain. Golf is more than a game, it is a sweet parcel of time for the players to "smell the roses" and commune with nature: a rewarding retreat from today's business technology—and that includes cellular telephones. Many of the finest private clubs recognize the threat of a shot being interrupted, and thus, the order has come down: NO CELLULAR PHONES ALLOWED ON THE COURSE. The retreat of golf must be preserved, and we favor this policy.

Years ago George S. May had phones on most tee installations at the now defunct Tam O'Shanter course in a Chicago suburb. Not only did they destroy the sanctity of golf, they increased playing time to five hours per round. Heed the warning bell.

About Carts

If you have not driven a golf cart, it is advisable to ride a few times before attempting to drive.

When the cart is stopped along side a ball to be played, it is stopped to the right of the ball for right-handed players—left for left handers. Keep the cart about ten feet to the side of the player, never directly in back of him, and certainly not in front. Players getting out of a cart to proceed to play their ball walk in back of the stopped cart, not in front. To speed play, when you replace clubs in your bag, at the same time take the clubs you think you'll need next.

And finally keep carts at least 20 yards away from greens and green side bunkers. Take them to the next teeing area.

The Four-Hour Interview

D o you mean to tell me that people play a four-hour round of golf strictly thinking about business? Of course not. But consider this point: Business people attain success by being preoccupied with matters of business. That's their M.O. Their minds are programmed for new data input and your actions on the golf course increase their database with pertinent information about you. Rare is the person who wipes his mental slate absolutely clean of business matters and is able to concentrate totally on just the fun of it all. They may claim, "I play golf to forget business." That is only a pathetic hope, not a fact. My point is that you will come under the subconscious scrutiny of business leaders on the golf course, and this book's point is that you can make the most of what we call *the four-hour interview,* the maximum time it should take for a round of golf.

What makes me think you'll be playing with business people and business leaders? No matter what research you read, golf's major participants are business people. Like it or not, men are still the major force in golf and in business, making most of the business decisions. Won't these hot shots only be playing private clubs? Not all the time. And this is where you come in. Your happy hunting grounds can even be public links, and plenty of business people will be there along with you. Only 11 percent of all golfers belong to private clubs. But it's likely that this 11 percent plays a leadership role in big business.

Are business leaders really out there on the golf course scouting personnel? Most of them can't help it. It's ingrained, though they may be the last to admit it. You just can't live in a corporate environment for the majority of your days and then shuck it aside completely when playing a round of golf. Yes, the business leaders you will bump into—and don't take that literally—will be knowingly or unknowingly weighing just how well you fit the executive mold. What is your confidence factor? Are you composed or are you throwing clubs and balls in anger like a juvenile? Do you seem to have specific goals in your play? Do you keep score with integrity and honesty? Are you aggressive? Are you responsible? Okay—let's put it another way. Can you add the number of your strokes? Do you cheat? Do you shake and stumble and seem unsure of when and what to do next? Do you dress in an oddball style, show up in dirty white shoes, peds, cut-off jeans? Do you know all the rules—or at least the basic ones? Did you show up on time? Do you appear happy? Are you visibly shaken by the stress of a short putt? Are you an excessive gambler? Do you appear to be planning your shots? Are you a risk-taker? Do you calculate risks well—*around* the water or *over* the water? What's your energy level? How good is your grammar? Are you a communicator? What's your basic personality? Are you grossly overweight? Do you need a haircut? Do you show any evidence of formal education? I seriously doubt that there would be a business leader on the golf course who would admit to making all of these observations about a fellow competitor. But I contend that these appraisals happen automatically. Subconsciously. One can't hang around closely with a person 'for four hours without forming some very definite opinions about him. So the image is formed, the die is cast!

Imagine for a moment the tremendous sales impact one can create in rendering professional service. The stock broker. The insurance salesperson. The accountant. What is *really* "for sale" in the services business? How can one differentiate the similarity of product? By judging the characteristics of the person representing the professional product. Where can personal values and integrity best be showcased? Where better than on the golf course? Attributes that promote trust—and get customers—are better conveyed in person than through two dozen direct-mail solicitations. Presuming a service is "par for the course," the representative's *image* is the *only* difference. This can attract a customer. This can determine a sale. What a fantastic opportunity! Almost every player is a prospect. To put the shoe on the other foot, if *you* were a potential customer, what better way than a round of golf to gain a keen insight into whether a fellow player belongs on your "leader board" of life.

By realizing the potential business implications golf holds for you, it's likely that you'll keep your eye on various charity events that occur in your county—The Boy Scout Tournament, Big Brothers, YMCA, hospital benefits, etcetera. Most often these events are held on public courses, but whether on public or private courses, you can easily find out who's holding what and where. And your application to play, along with the prescribed donation—anywhere from fifty to a few hundred dollars—assure you a berth in one of these golf charity events. Corporations are the big donors to this type of event. Their top officers will definitely participate. Charity events are an opportunity to expand your visibility in the business community and get to know on a social basis many of the influentials.

Through golf tournaments, golfers raise more money for charities, according to leading journals, than any other special group in the United States. Corporations encourage their qualified officers to participate. By paying (donating) for their playing spots in Pro-Am events, and every kind of civic and charitable golf tournament, golfers contribute to one of the largest fundraising activities in America.

Let's take a moment to explain the term Pro-Am. You know that the Professional Golfers Association has a tour that runs the majority of the year around the country. Probably some major PGA event is played in or near your city. Usually on a Wednesday, the day before the actual Pro tournament starts, the pros are grouped with amateur entries (such as yourself) who have paid a fee to play on this special day. It's a competitive event, where one pro normally plays with three or four amateurs, all of whom donated money to get a *slot,* a playing place, in the Pro-Am. These playing slots may be by invitation, but normally are on a first-come, first-served basis. Applications are made sometimes months or a year in advance by amateurs who wish to participate. The stipend is usually pretty heavy for a day of golf—but you automatically win some prizes, called *tee prizes,* just for showing up. It's an event you may wish to participate in if you're seeking high visibility in the civic and business community where you live. Your local pro shop can fill you in on the particulars.

These functions may not be held at private country clubs alone, and they attract the skilled as well as the unskilled, but they are a great proving ground where behavior separates business barons from the bunglers.

Aside from this opportunity, there's always a cadre of business golfers playing public courses who may be awaiting their application acceptance at one or more of the exclusive private country clubs. And Starters, those gentlemen at public courses who are in charge of who tees off when, may blend you in with other business types on any given day of the week you intend to play.

You remember, don't you, when they asked the infamous bank robber Willie Sutton why he robbed banks? He replied, "Because that's where the money is." Well, just translate that philosophy into why you play golf and you'll be putting everything in the right perspective.

It's a given that if you pursue golf actively it is virtually impossible to not run into and play with important business types who can easily influence your future. Taken as gospel, the way you play can produce invaluable business contacts:

- Employment
- Corporate promotion
- Sales
- VIP referrals
- International connections
- Your acceptance into the world of big business

I've always been amazed at the number of ladder-climbing business executives who finally concede that golf is a must, then ignore the good manners of golf and botch promotions, impair important business relationships, and even lose friendships because of their actions on a golf course.

Our goal is to see to it that as many good opinions as possible will be formed about you. If all this causes you to hope to knock it in the woods and stay there, take heart.

♀ You and I are in this thing together! Where you're going, I've been. We are side by side, and I'll stick right by you to help you get ready for, and through, a complete round of golf. I'll be your invisible sidekick, friend, and partner.

But questions may be stinging your mind. Do I tell them that I'm a novice? How do I introduce myself? What if they ask what I do? Do I bring up the subject of business? These are such immediate questions that we should talk about them here and now.

Certainly you will introduce yourself and you will find that among players, *after* introductions, it's a first name game. "I'm Joe Wellington and (if you're just starting out) very much of a novice at the game, but I'll try to move right along without delay, so that you gentlemen will enjoy your day." No, you don't belabor the point that you are a beginner, if you are one. Everyone had to start sometime, and already you've shown that you will make every attempt to be considerate of your fellow players. Score one for you and our side.

There's a very good chance that someone will ask where you live and what you do. Give them the general area of where you live, and tell them your particular career category or, if you like, the company you work for. "I'm basically a sales type—enjoy sales, but seem to be involved in administration right now. I hope to get fully involved in sales one of these days soon. I believe that's where I belong." 'Nuff said. We're trolling. You'll have to figure out the best way to toss off the details about what you're doing now and what you hope to be doing in the future in a most casual way. It's very likely that the others will volunteer their general residential area, perhaps their firm, and what they do. Most often this seems to naturally evolve as the camaraderie builds, either pre-game or on the course.

But what if you find out that none of the people you're playing with have the authority or the responsibility regarding decisions involving hire and fire? Ostensibly, there's nothing they can do for you. Or is there? If the net impression is that they like you, they'll remember you. The very worst that can happen is that three more people will be able to carry your name and your message later to someone who may count. Maybe you said somewhere in the course of the game that you happen, by experience, to know one helluva lot about lumber, but that you're really not putting that experience to good use. A point made just may stick. And it may come back in some way to help you.

But should you then, at every opportunity, bring up business? Egads, no! You'll be acting like a jerk if you do.

I remember one time playing with a bookkeeper-type, and on the very first hole he said to a fellow competitor who was obviously big business, "Well, you put that right into the hole—and say, speaking of being in the hole, I'd like to tell you about a time that I took a deficit—an absolute liability—and turned it into a tremendous asset for my company." Heaven forbid such a bore.

Well then, how *does* business talk originate? There's no sure-fire answer to that one. Waiting between shots—and I'm afraid there's too much of that—and presuming that you're playing with strangers, it tends to evolve, somehow, someplace. You can bet on it. But it can be instigated easily, if you're clever. If a gentleman says, "This hole reminds me of one I played quite often in Florida," ask, "Do you have a business in Florida or just travel there quite a bit for the fun of it?" That will provoke some information. Another good but obtuse way of garnering information is to make some comment about a business item you saw on the business pages of your newspaper. If you can, end with a question, "It looks like a pretty big deal, doesn't it?" You've started the business ball rolling.

Some readers may think all this is pretty crass, but I would like to see you position yourself to the best advantage—on the golf course and in business. You see, even mentioning that you read a business article says you are a businessman. It says you're current. It says chances are you're educated. It says you may be in a line of business which provokes another person's thinking. You're informed, you've communicated, you've put a bit of personality on display that's not all wrapped up in you, the individual. You've become a conduit of things involving business. And whether it's a business item in the newspaper, or one of the many business-motivated, best-seller books that you allude to in the way of small talk, you've established a presence. You've established interest in yourself beyond your actual ability at the game.

But you might be saying, "Boy, if I could only play well, it would be so much easier." Yes and no. It's certainly a big advantage to be able to play average golf, which you can do with some dedicated practice and some lessons.

But let's take a moment to look at the opposite side of the coin. You play exceptionally well! You are an absolute whiz on the golf course! You are pro material! This, quite easily, can communicate such things as, "Since he's this good, he must not have to work, is not interested in work, or spends damn little time working." It's been said that many of the greatest golfers either had no business ambition other than golf, or they were already so rich through inheritance that they did not need to think about anything but golf. So you see, the great golfer, in a business environment, can immediately become suspect. Now, if a person happens to have played golf in school, or learned it as a caddie, then people will often say, "He's good at it because he established the foundation of his game in his younger years." So, that's okay.

The great moment of truth that is so encouraging is that although you don't want to be the worst of golfers, being among the very best *can* have its drawbacks. If the message you are learning is that you need not be a great golfer in order to realize great business benefits from the game, then you get an "A" in attitude and a "P" for perfect perception.

Here are some things to keep in mind:

• We should promote fast play. Slow play is a round of golf that exceeds four hours. Intolerable! Unacceptable! We'll share some of the time savers that can make the game happier for you and for those who play with you.

• We have a responsibility for the care of the golf course, such as replacing divots in the landscape—replacing the sod that your club head has snapped into the air after a crisp, satisfying shot.

• We also wholeheartedly believe that a player should look to his local club pro for lessons as opposed to the buddy-buddy system of learning.

And all the while there are great friendships that can be developed as each of us seeks to find the elusive secrets of playing better.

And while we search together, I offer to you more than forty-five years' experience in playing around the world, on all kinds of golf courses with all types of people. We'll have some fun together, hopefully walking the fairways with a breeze to our backs.

Kinds of
Golf Courses

L et's take a minute to categorize clubs and courses. There are public courses, semi-private clubs, resort courses, military courses, private golf clubs, and private country clubs. The beehive that has the most honey is the private country club, simply because the bulk of the upper echelon business people play and belong there.

The king, of course, is the private golf club. It's a breed apart. There are more to be found in the East and they have one sole function: golf. Pine Valley, just outside Philadelphia, typifies them for me. It is hallowed and sanctified. Its clubhouse is classically understated. As I walked into the library there, with its old leather, high-backed chairs, I noted folded newspapers on a side stand. I fully expected to turn to a front page and see something bannered there like this:

"As it was in the beginning, is now and ever shall be. . . ."

9

The players of private golf clubs are rarely emerging golfers. They've already arrived. It's a whole different experience. Much of the membership is nonresident, and the qualifications for membership go far beyond the means of money, but have to do with pedigree, and the likes of the Fortune 500.

Minding your manners has just as much application on a municiple course as it does at a private club. The biggest difference is that good behavior is not just admirable at a private club, it can make or break you.

There's an abundance of misinformation about how one goes about obtaining membership in a private country club. Let me skim the details for you. It's not money alone as many think. Yes, it takes money and it is expensive. There's normally a substantial joining fee, dues, minimum expenditures for food and beverage, etcetera. But much has to do with the social acceptance of the individual. An applicant needs references to support his moral character, affability, integrity, plus testimonial references from three or more members of that club's existing membership. Questions to those giving references include, "Have you ever entertained this person in your home?" "Have you met his wife?" "Would you enjoy a foursome with both of them?" "Would you recommend the applicant to your best friends as a player in their foursome?" "Would you intend to introduce them to other members?" "Do you know about his financial responsibility?" (Can he and does he pay his bills or is he a deadbeat?)

The questions go on and on and the point here is that they reflect on the person, the person's behavior, and the person's social adaptability. Not one question about how good a player he or she is.

If your aspiration is membership in a private country club, chances are you will be asked there as a guest a few times before that subject becomes front-burner. You will be under the observation glass if you are a potential candidate for membership.

Country clubs are now attempting to balance their membership with socially acceptable people, not just the old, retired, and rich. Clubs know they need vitality, youth, aggressiveness, and lots of variety. Well-mannered variety without discrimination.

Being a good guest at a private country club is merely a matter of being properly prepared, and we'll cover that subject adequately. You know, there are those who wouldn't think of attending a company officers' meeting or participating in a sales or management seminar, without meticulous preparation. They learn all the unwritten innuendos of behavior that abound with business/political overtones. Well, that's the kind of preparation we're going for in golf.

Preparation saves us from ever becoming a "Bob Bungler" or "Bobbie," if you'd like, for women face very similar dilemmas and opportunities in golf.

According to *Business Week,* women now account for 40 percent of all new players. Two-thirds of these five million plus are employed and believe that "you can build business relationships on the golf course."

WISE WORDS FROM A WISE WOMAN

As of 1991 Val Skinner had three victories in her eight years on the LPGA Tour. She had this to say in *Golf News* about starting the clock when it is clearly your turn to play: "I feel forty-five seconds is adequate time to take for a shot." The count begins when it becomes your turn to play and concludes when your ball comes to rest. "Golf to me is a game of momentum. Peak performance is when you get in the zone and you can keep the pace and keep it going. Everybody is going to play better. You should evaluate on the way to the golf ball what your next play is going to be. Don't start when you get there. Have a game plan."

Three
Assumptions

1. You have elected to go to the course—any course—and you are aware that, by the way you act, your image is on the line. You want to do it right, even if it's your first time out. Your aspirations include the possibility of joining a private club, thus you want your preparation to be meticulous.
2. You have the equipment to play and have had at least some lessons from a professional on how to play the game.
3. You have read the abridged book of Rules of Golf. There are thirty-four rules and hundreds of subclauses, as well as exceptions. A golf or pro shop will carry the USGA pocket-sized rule book, and it usually sells for $1.

You just cannot skip over reading and understanding the rules. Here's a couple of tips:

- Match Play means you are playing a fellow competitor by the hole. (If you've won the first two holes you're plus two.) Read the rules as they pertain to Match Play. You'll probably be playing this most often.

- In Stroke Play (also called Medal Play), count your total strokes versus your competitors' total strokes. Penalties vary significantly between Match Play and Stroke Play.

The rest of this story, then, is how you go about it. And we want to go about it without embarrassment. We will not eat dinner with a spoon.

It's said that everyone plays three games of golf for every round played:

1. The game we intend to play.
2. The actual game played.
3. The game we wish we had played.

As to any one of the three, breathe deeply, take heart, and believe me when I say I have never seen gentlemen or ladies throw fits over a high-scoring, beginning player. The fits fly over the player who violates etiquette.

That's the crux of the game of golf.

Getting Ready
for the Game

W hite athletic socks for gentlemen are out. I don't know why. Don't ask. I start with this trivia to make the point that there are a number of do's and don'ts that escape explanation. In the main, however, do's and don'ts can and will be explained.

We'll start with a dress rehearsal. Looking the part.

Prior to being "fine fellow, well met," thank goodness for a little contemplative time about the game coming up.

Clubs and courses vary in their dress codes. If you're being hosted, it is quite proper for you to ask your host about dress codes before arriving. Jogging outfits, track or tennis shorts, even certain golf shoes with funny rubber bubbles on the soles are definitely out.

Men can hardly go wrong with slacks (the wild stripes and checks are out of vogue at this writing), a golf shirt (*not* a T- shirt), and a golf hat, if that is to your liking. Sweater and/or foul weather gear should also be considered. Knickers, by the way, are making a fashionable comeback. On the golf course itself, the golf shirt is never, ever removed, even if it's 115 degrees in the shade.

Women are basically safe attired in a knee length skirt. Culottes two to three inches above the knee are also usually acceptable. Other attire includes golf blouse, sweater, and a provision for foul weather. Again, a hat is optional. Some private clubs also favor peds, others prefer below-the-knee socks. Many reject slacks. Flat shoes only, with or without spikes, are the order of the day for all courses. Such things as jeans and tennis shorts—yes, even if you are just going to watch—are off limits.

A couple of years back, I asked one of my female employees to deliver some business papers to me at the prestigious Los Angeles Country Club, where I was a guest of a close friend, Chuck Young. She did so by the main club entrance, attired in jeans, T-shirt, and western boots. A fetching figure on the streets of Beverly Hills; for shame at the L.A. Country Club. Unfortunately, this resulted in a reprimand to my host and an embarrassment to me. I should have had better presence of mind. "Sticky wicket" is a private club's prerogative.

Tradition, being an integral part of the game, holds that on any golf course the acceptability of apperance is a big part of the etiquette of golf.

Now, your other consideration is whether you'll be staying for dinner or another social activity that will take you into the dining room area of the clubhouse. If so, you'll want to bring slacks, jacket, and either a dress shirt and tie or casual shirt—along with a change of socks, of course. Comparable dinner wardrobe applies for women as well. A garment bag is not a bad idea at all, unless you are sure the plan is to hit the ball and then hit the highway. All this has particular emphasis at a private country club, where being well dressed is essential.

What does well dressed actually mean? Look for the middle ground. Not too flashy, not too "poly," but clean and pressed with a conservative sports outfit. Take a tip from watching the pros on the PGA tour on TV. They know their image is not only on display on the course, but nationwide. Or pick up a golf magazine for pointers.

The radical mistake can be to wear business pants that are too worn looking for business occasions and are "elected" as golf slacks. They'll look like just what they are: has-beens. The other radical mistake is the "beach boy" look. The shirt is always tucked inside the pants and the golf shirt has a soft collar.

Until you get a feel for how others dress, you're better off being conservative than flamboyant. Some may say "safe is establishment." You got it! That's where we're headed. And that's the game we're going to win.

There is a great deal of concern, especially among beginners, about the type of equipment and clubs they play with. Here are some guidelines on that subject. First of all, let's start with the bag. It can be big or small or any color, so long as it's not ripped, torn, or ratty looking. It doesn't have to be one of those oversized pro bags to properly impress people. As a matter of fact, there's an old Texas expression that says of the novice player who comes to the course trotting out the huge pro bag, "Aw bet that guy is all bag." Meaning, that is all the talent he's got. A decent-looking bag of modest size is a smart investment. I don't recommend hand-me-downs.

Now on to clubs. Keep concentrating on the fact that I'm concerned primarily with your image, not necessarily with which model club fits you the best. That's a pro's job. We want you to have head covers for your woods. When you want to take out the driver for use, you take the head cover off and when you put the driver back in the bag the head cover goes back on. It protects the club from dirt, ding marks, and moisture and makes you look like a seasoned golfer. No head covers, no couth.

I strongly suggest that you have clubs that match. That means you don't have a Wilson 2-iron, a Spaulding 6-iron, a Ladies' 8-iron, and a Cobra wedge. It's not important that you have every type of club ever manufactured in your bag, but it is important to your appearance, as well as to your game, that you have most clubs that match. Same make, same model.

In my estimation it would be pretty hard to score adequately without a driver, a 3-wood, a 5- or 7-wood, a 4- through 9-iron, a pitching wedge, a sand wedge, and a putter. The competitive events usually dictate that the player carry no more than fourteen clubs. Otherwise, I carry fifteen and it appears to me that most people carry fifteen or sixteen clubs. A great dichotomy: People want to sell you all those clubs and then when it comes to a hard-core competitive event, they insist that you carry no more than fourteen. On the other hand, I suppose if there weren't some rule about it, there would be golfers with a U-Haul trailing behind them, loaded with every type of club known to man. Make sure the facings of your clubs are clean. This is not only aesthetically pleasing, but it's practical as well.

If you're wondering where to buy your clubs, let's take a moment for that. The discount houses usually have prices below the pro shop or golf shop prices at the various courses and clubs. But at the risk of angering a few people, I believe the place to buy your equipment is from your home pro: the professional at the course you play. You should be fitted properly, and the pros are better qualified to do this for you. Even if his prices are a few modest dollars more, remember you'll be looking to him for lessons, friendly tips, starting times, or maybe just a warm, encouraging smile. I believe strongly that it's a two-way street: You support your pro and he supports you. Someday when you're very anxious to get paired on the golf course with that Mr., Ms., or Mrs. So-and-So who could be mighty important to you in business, it would be nice to have the pro arrange such a game and care about your well-being. This is more likely to happen if you've given your pro your support. There's nothing wrong with the discounter's merchandise, generally speaking. But since we're trying to do everything the right way, I think that golf equipment purchased from your pro is the way to go.

One day I was playing an exclusive private country club with a dentist who I knew had a six-figure income. This dude was playing with X-out balls—bargain balls from the discounters where the trade name had to be crossed out because they did not measure up to the quality standards of the manufacturer. No good for you. You're a business person and you want to reflect that you place a high priority on quality. That's why you will not tee up with an obviously inferior golf ball.

What about renting clubs or shoes? It's all right. Particularly all right if you're playing a course far from home. I know good executive golfers who travel from coast to coast and intend to play only once, if the occasion arises. They will rent from the pro at the course, who usually keeps a spare bag full, and a few shoes available. Let's not do that while we're in our home territory, however. That projects much too tentative an attitude, which could indicate a lack of proper preparation.

Here's another question which should be answered: Does it cost anything for you as a guest to play a private club? No, it probably won't cost *you,* but it surely will cost your host. He's paid out a considerable sum, perhaps up to 100,000 dollars or more, after being recommended, interviewed, and voted on, to join the club. That membership money merely pays for his and his wife's privilege of playing. He pays green fees for you, approximately 35 to 150 dollars, plus the cost of your cart and whatever you eat and drink. After paying for membership, he pays dues, a house minimum to encourage his eating and drinking activity, locker fee, range fee, etcetera. So you are a guest.

What about fees on a public course? Let's presume you've been called and invited to play by another golfer. Ordinarily, this does not mean that he intends to be your host. It means you pay your own way and that he merely would enjoy your company. It's better when you check in at the course to tell the person in charge the party you're to play with and whip out the billfold for your round of golf and your 50 percent fee for the cart (if you're taking a cart). If you want to be big about it, you can pick up the whole tab for the cart. The point is that the preferred etiquette is for each person to pay his own way, and whatever the cart rental is, that it be split 50-50 between the driver and the rider.

When you decided to play, you were probably told a starting time, if the course happens to be that crowded. It's a pretty good rule of thumb to plan to arrive forty-five minutes before tee time, especially at a private club. There you have some checking in to do. A locker to locate. The pre-game Grill—covered in a later chapter. And you may wish to hit a few practice balls prior to teeing off, presuming the course has a practice range.

If you have not been to the course before, you will have to locate the unloading zone. At some private clubs, you pull up right in front and there is someone to remove your clubs from the trunk and park your car. Other clubs handle this process in back of the club and closer to the first tee.

Parking is usually well indicated after you've determined whether you're a front, side, or rear door arrival.

Unless you are *positive* there is no locker room, changing one's shoes in the parking lot is definitely bad form.

Cogitate for a few minutes over the pros and cons of taking a caddie (if there are caddies) as opposed to riding in a cart. Notice I said *riding*. Do not volunteer to *drive* a cart if you are going on a strange course. You will not be sure where to park the carts or what paths the carts should follow, and there's a lot of "local knowledge" about this. Of course, a cart is not driven within 20 yards of a green—but instead is driven to the next teeing area following the hole that you're playing. The driver should know about going forward, backing up, setting the brake properly, and be quite aware of the potential danger of tipping over when navigating hilly terrain.

I remember playing a couple of years back at Banff, up in Canada. Gorgeous course. The golf shop's procedure was to charge a huge deposit on the cart when you checked it out. This floored me! I asked their reasoning. "A lot of people are checking out carts who have never driven one before. Unfortunately, we found the carts wrapped around trees or used to ford creeks and lakes. The potential damage is excessive."

I was about to see the proof in the pudding. On the Number One tee, we were to follow two visiting Japanese. They were freshly arrived from Tokyo and had no motorized cart experience whatsoever. Both hit rather nice tee shots off Number One. But, for *one* golfer, that would be his last stroke for all of that particular vacation. As one jumped into the cart, the other was walking in front of the cart. The driver hit the accelerator. The Japanese in front bit the dust. And we saw him for the next few days riding along with his pal, his broken arm in a sling.

I don't think it hurt the cart that much. Might have though, had it hit a tree. Which proves, I guess, there can be all kinds of broken limbs and carts. Anyway, no matter who's driving, carts can be dangerous.

It may well be that if it's a private club, they will assign at least one forecaddie to your foursome, even if you elect to take carts. He's normally responsible for being up ahead of you and watching where the balls land, assisting you with your putts, and raking the traps, and will most often hand carry all putters for his foursome.

As to the proposition of taking individual caddies, we should decide to do what the other three players of your foursome desire to do. If they elect to take caddies, which will probably be discussed in the social encounter in a Grill Room prior to teeing off, you should also. If you have some physical affliction inhibiting your walking 18 holes, it is perfectly within reason that you explain your physical impairment and request a cart.

There are a couple other methods of getting oneself around the golf course. One has to do with carrying your own bag. And the second one has to do with renting or bringing a pull cart. A few comments about each.

For a long time, carrying your own bag was considered tacky, and it still is at many private clubs. However, with the physical fitness craze, and at certain hours, even many private clubs are relaxing their views toward this and are permitting it more liberally.

As to pull carts. Most courses okay them. Some private clubs allow and will even store pull carts for men and women. As an example, many fine courses in the northwestern part of the United States provide the pull cart option. The basic reason behind this is that, as the caddie is vanishing, and due to the incessant rainfall in the Northwest, greens superintendents sometimes prohibit the electric or gasoline cart because the slushing around they do causes excessive turf damage. Thus the pull cart alternative.

If either alternative, carrying your own or using a pull cart, appeals to you, it is something you may wish to look into. Generally speaking it should not become a preferred option of yours at a private club.

A note about carts: In Hawaii, it's almost 100 percent carts, and the private club other than military is rare, with the most notable exception being Wailai on Oahu, home of the Hawaiian Open.

About caddies: They're a vanishing breed. If you're lucky enough to have them, protect them. Be kind to them. Caddie flogging went out about a hundred years ago. (Can you imagine that? It's in the golf history books. Hit a bad shot, beat the hell out of your caddie.)

Unload the bag of the non-necessities. We don't carry dozens of balls. Nothing infuriates a caddie more than to be packing two or three dozen balls that will never be used. Make sure that your bag has an adequate shoulder strap on it, wide enough so that it doesn't cut into his flesh. Introduce yourself to your caddie by saying you are Mr., Ms., or Mrs. So-and-So. He will announce his name, probably his first name, and this is the name by which you will address him.

We won't want to embarrass ourselves or our caddies by asking them what club to hit. Since they are not golf professionals, we don't look to them for professional advice. The club professional has advised them not to attempt to play pro. When a caddie is asked certain wrong questions, he's being asked to compromise a conduct principle. "Am I swinging too fast?" "Why am I slicing the ball?" Don't do it. He may, out of sheer pity somewhere along the line, make a slight suggestion, which can be taken with a kind "thank you."

Feel perfectly free to ask him yardage; then you must determine what club you should hit.

It's my opinion that the following is a must *before* ever actually playing. Hit your 5-iron. Hit it until you've hit it fairly well. Then step off the yardage. Let's just presume you hit it 150 yards.

Now you will know to add or subtract on club use when you find a yardage marker, usually placed on flat water spigots at numerous places along the fairway. Example: Every iron club gives you about a ten to twelve yard variance. So, if the yardage marker you see says 160 yards, then that suggests a 4-iron. If it says 140, that suggests a 6-iron (shorter than the 5-iron in distance). It's trickier with 9-irons and wedges—depending on full-swing shots or half-swing shots. It will help you immensely to test out average yards you attain with your woods as well— but your first key is the distance you get with your 5-iron.

We mustn't ask golfing advice of an opponent or an opponent's caddie. 'Tis against the rules to ask your opponent or his caddie. Not only against the rules, with penalties, it's "Bob

Bungler" golf. Your caddie or experienced partner can give you all of the terrain advice that you need. Hit it left. It will probably bounce right. Fine. "It's full carry." He's advising you to use a little bit more club because the green is elevated, and more distance than is apparent is required.

These tips can be invaluable to you—"local knowledge" as to the geographic characteristics of the golf course.

Many times I have seen a relative newcomer discuss over and over with his caddie or his partner how much a ball will break on the green when it is struck towards the hole. One can only tell the amount of break by the *speed* of the putt. And only the striker of the ball knows how hard the putt will be hit. It is logical to ask your caddie or playing partner only, "Does this ball break left to right or right to left?" The answer may be something like, "It's a rather *radical* break from left to right," or "There's a *slight* break from left to right."

Your caddie or partner may also tell you whether you're going uphill with the grain or against the grain (against the grain you hit it harder), or may make a general statement like, "it's slick" or "it's slow." One shouldn't ask how slick or how slow, or how much left or how much right. Again, it presumes anyone will know how hard you're going to hit the putt, thus the speed of your putt. A person asking these questions is delaying the game and displaying very bad form.

Consider the following: The harder the putt is hit, the less the break. If you intend to strike a dying putt, then you would wish to play more break. Discussing these things *ad infinitum* is a bore, and certainly not in keeping with the etiquette of golf.

I have found that most better players will attempt to read their putt by either squatting behind it—walking the terrain between their ball and the cup to get a feel for undulation— or by plumbing the putt (a practice far overdone by your average player, but one that has been fostered by watching golf on the tube).

Now let's do a final check on our equipment. You have a bag and clubs, and an ample number of balls. A half a dozen ought to do it unless you're mighty wild or playing a course in the Wild Kingdom. How about a glove? Do you have tees? Ball markers?

You may well be asking yourself, "Where do I get these?" Gloves and balls cost money, no matter where, and if you were to pick them up at a private club, it's very likely that they will not accept your cash, but charge the item to your host's account. The better idea is to get these things in advance. At a private club, *tees* and *ball markers* are given to you as a courtesy. At a public course, they're available in the golf shop at a very modest charge. You'll need them so make it a rule to have some. All part of proper preparation, which is frankly making a statement about you. It says that in business you wouldn't go off half-cocked. You'd be ready.

Time out for a cute story about rules. Paul Runyan is one of the revered names in professional golf. Paul was a tremendous tournament player, establishing umpteen national records, and is renowned for his teaching abilities. A masterful short game artist. Anyway, he was the head professional at La Jolla Country Club at the time of this story. Paul was first and foremost always the gentleman. He addressed all members by "Mister" or "Missus" (this was before Ms.), and he had the delicate art of being extremely courteous to all members without being subservient. Even good golfers get confused from time to time about the intricacies of the rules. They storm the pro shop, badger the head pro, and lay down an ultimatum as to whether they are right or their opponent is right in an interpretation of the rules. (Breaking rules costs you penalty strokes. Bad news.)

Paul would find himself in the delicate situation of having to take sides for this member or that when accurately interpreting the rule book. One day he declared, "When any of you members have a question about a ruling, please come to me without using the name of the players involved. Just refer to Player A and Player B. Then I'll look up the ruling and tell you what it is." Fair enough. The next day a member stormed in with a dispute. He said to Paul, "All right, here's the problem. We were on hole Number three, over by the fence, where the ball had come to rest. Now my question is this. Player A, who happens to be a sonofabitch, wants to know . . ." I don't know how Paul handled it. But I'm sure he did well. He never bogeyed good manners.

One of the key questions that will be asked prior to the game will be, "What's your handicap?" You either have one or you don't. The answer is never, "I think about a ___." Most public courses can offer a golfer, for a small fee, the opportunity to have a handicap determined by the United States Golf Association. There are even some correspondence computer centers that advertise from time to time in golf magazines that can assist you. Without going into detail, a handicap is determined by averaging your 10 lowest scores out of your last 20 rounds—give or take some ingredients like course ratings (slope)—and a stroke percentage deduction, giving you an index that translates into a handicap.

In days gone by, every player had just a "handicap." The United States Golfing Association declared this unfair. What if you got your handicap on a very difficult course (high slope) and I got mine on an easy course (low slope). So all courses now have slope ratings to result in more accurate handicaps, making competition more equitable. All in all, you need to know the slope of the course you're playing on and your index. Remember your index. When you go to an "away course," just check your index against their slope rating and that will translate into your handicap at that course.

If you don't have a handicap, three things can happen. There are a couple of handicap scoring systems that can be invoked called the Callaway Handicapping System and the Peoria System. (Nobody I know from Peoria knows where the hell this name came from.)

But you'll probably run into a congenial crowd, eager for your money, who will ask you what your last few scores have been and where you played. Someone in your group will probably suggest that you play at such and such handicap, depending upon those past scores. This will all happen *before* golf partners are established, so as to keep partnerships unbiased. You may say, for instance, "The average of my last four or five scores has been 96." If par on the course you are about to play is 72, they then would subtract 72 from 96 leaving 24, and they will probably adjust this downward, 22 or 23, and will likely be a bit generous if this is your first time on the course. What does this mean?

Look at a score card. Any score card. You will note that where it says "Hole Number One," several other bits of information are to be found directly underneath. How long the hole is, what par is on the hole. Someplace down below, the par and the handicap for women will be listed. If the first hole is a handicap 10, and everyone is playing to a full handicap, you would receive a stroke on that hole. If you take 6, then that would become a net 5. Presuming the 22 handicap, it's easy to calculate—on the holes handicapped 1, 2, 3, and 4, you would receive two strokes against your gross on each of these holes. So that if you shot a 7, it would be a net 5. But this will all be up to the scorekeeper to calculate once your handicap is established. What may well occur, is that your foursome may play off the lowest handicap player in the group, commonly called a low-ball match.

In this case, if the lowest handicap player were to be a 10, you subtract 10 from your 22 and you would receive 12 strokes where they fall on the scorecard—meaning the holes that are handicapped the toughest from 1 through 12.

You don't have to be a whiz at this type of thing unless you're very experienced. If you're new, you definitely should not even try to keep general score for all players. And this will all become clearer to you after the game when you're paying up or being paid off. I certainly don't want to indicate that there will be gambling involved in your little get-together, but it would be fairly close to miraculous if there were not some wagering.

When I was a novice, I got very little explanation about the gambling details and have since found out that all novices suffer the same fate. I think the reason for this is that it's just too damn tough to explain. Too many variations.

Gambling is different geographically and it's even a bit different from course to course. I sometimes suspect that about half the players don't understand the wagering until it's payoff or collection time. Why are we so bashful about asking for these details? I suppose it's for the same reason that no one likes to admit in Las Vegas that they don't know how to shoot craps. Well, I take a different view of it on the golf course. There always appears to be one authority in each foursome. If nothing else, he's louder about it than anyone else. Go ahead and ask questions. The only dumb question is the one you don't ask. Face right up to it if you don't understand it. Say something like, "Look, I want to do this right. In order to do that, I have to understand it. And I don't. Take me through it a step at a time so I can enjoy it as much as you do." I think that's just a whole helluva lot better than faking it and getting trapped by displaying ignorance later on. Let's remember our "image" thing. Before you sign a contract, you want to know the contents, right? Well, it's not all *that* serious but I think it's pretty cowardly for someone to agree to the conditions of a contest without knowing how come or what for. The bottom line is that a person gets more respect by asking questions than by just bobbing his head up and down.

Along your golfing way, I suspect you will find a peculiarity about wagering. It's been my experience that the richer the club and the more affluent its club membership, the less dollar amount is wagered. What's really on the line is ego. Perhaps there is so much money there that money is less important. Or maybe it's like the white athletic socks: I don't know. Don't ask. But if you've gathered that you should bring along a little extra cash, you've got that right.

As someone once said, if you can't afford the game, don't play it. It's one of my favorite expressions because it was first uttered to me by a late dear friend at La Jolla Country Club, Joe Suffudy. The situation was as follows: Joe was a very high handicapper and a great benefactor to the golf ball companies of the world. A dozen lost balls per round was somewhat commonplace with dear Joe.

Joe, like all of us, sometimes found an early point of exasperation with the game and it happened to him on hole Number 13. He knocked his ball from the tee out of bounds. Rather than return to his bag for another ball, he called to his playing partner in the cart to throw him a ball. It was his partner's habit to buy a sleeve of three new balls each time before he played. So the friendly partner threw Joe one of his three brand-new balls. Joe knocked it out of bounds, then turned and said, "Throw me another ball." Joe knocked that one out of bounds.

Joe turned and said, "Throw me another ball." His partner said, "Good God, Joe, these are brand-new balls." Joe fixed him with a steely glare in the eye and said, "If you can't afford the game, don't play it."

Before I forget, it was also Joe who coined another one of my favorite phrases of golf. When, upon completing his 18th hole, someone asked Joe how it went, he replied, "This is the worst good time I've ever had."

It seems that every club has a few memorable characters like Joe. Each club has The Nifty Dresser. Mr. Gripes and Moans. The Hustler. And of course, legends abound from club to club. In ensuing chapters, I'll invite you to meet a number of these characters, for better or for worse.

Now, let's review some of your other basics before proceeding to the course. Yes, a *whiff*—when you miss the ball entirely—does count as a stroke. No, you can't just drop a ball where you think you lost one or where it went out of bounds. If you had any doubt you should have played a *provisional* ball, and short of that you must *return to the tee,* or from wherever you struck the ball O.B. or lost it. But you know these basic things, don't you? Because in our earlier assumptions we listed that you should be familiar with at least the abridged version of the rules.

One of the demonics of the game is slow play. Yes, those fellas on TV are certainly slow on the green. However, remember it probably took them fewer strokes to arrive at the green. You will certainly want to avoid slow play. And I mean there are *slow* players. I've seen prisoners walk faster on their way to the electric chair.

As mentioned before, a four-hour round for 18 holes should be the maximum. There are a number of ways you can achieve this. If you are going to take such a high number of strokes on a particular hole as to eliminate you from competition, just declare your ball out of play and continue on "in pocket." Pick up the ball, put it in your pocket, and forget it.

Here are a couple of tips that can speed up play: When in a cart, put your club back in the bag while removing the next one you need. One action instead of two. Second, when you're taking out your *approach iron,* take your *putter* as well. One action instead of two.

You should have some idea how far your ball is from the hole. Generally there are 150-yard indicators in the form of shrubs, sprinklers—some yardage indicators that your fellow competitors will be happy to tell you about. If you're back of the 150 you add yardage. If you're short of the 150 you subtract yardage. If you know what club it is that you hit 150 yards, you're probably within a club or two of making your decision some 20 yards *before* you even get to your ball.

Depending on the lie of your ball it may be a 4-, 5- or 6-iron. If it's normally a 5-iron for you but you're into the wind, you may need a 4-iron. The point is, many of your decisions can be calculated before you arrive at the ball. As the old joke goes, "What do you hit from the 150-yard marker? Usually a 5-iron, two 7-irons, a 9-iron, and a wedge."

Another good pointer for a beginner is that if you dub the ball—hit a worm burner, some 20, 25, or 30 yards ahead of your last position—don't bother getting back into the cart. Stride briskly to it, all the while determining what yardage is left and what you are about to hit. You know the person farthest from the hole has the honor of hitting first. In golf it is said that he who is "away" always hits first. Keep alert. Look around you. When you're the farthest away from the flagstick, you know it's your turn. You don't need to be a golfer to know who's away—unless it's close to a tie. You can then ask, "Is it you or me?" Be ready for it.

Then we mustn't lollygag on the green. If another player is standing behind his ball lining up his putt, do not cross over in front of him. Walk to your place, walking *behind* him. If he were lining up a rifle shot to a target, would you walk in front, disturbing his concentration? He might be tempted to pull the trigger. Do not stand in his *vision line* as he looks forward or backward. Do your putting and move swiftly to the next tee. Slow play not only holds up the course, it holds up the people you're playing with. It can destroy their tempo—*vastly* important in golf—and try their patience beyond endurance. If your group is inadvertently causing slow play, be prepared on any particular hole to invite a faster playing group behind you to play through. That's the proper protocol in golf.

Play with your own equipment. Not only is it against the rules, but it's bad form to say something like, "I like the looks of your driver. May I give it a whack or two?" Sometimes clubs take on more of a personal relationship to the player than even his toothbrush. A player can see his shaft snapping, spike marks ground into his club head, or some similar disaster occurring.

Out there someplace, you may run across a bright shiny new ball that's not yours and obviously not one belonging to your foursome. "Oh what a break. I found a ball." No! Leave it! It may be one gone astray from another player behind that hill or back of those trees. Establish yourself. "I don't want something for nothing." Class!

Are you becoming fraught with trepidation? Don't be. We've all been through it. It's just a matter of preparation.

Let's review some common vocabulary that you're apt to hear on the course. After all, the vocabulary has been developing for 500 years. That's how long this bloody thing has been going on.

- *"It's your honor"* means, hit away, your time to play.
- *"We play in the leather"* means if, when putting, your ball comes to rest in an area between the hole and the leather of your putter—or the grip of your putter—that's a *gimme*. That means rather than having to putt it, you will consider having putted it by adding one more stroke to your score while picking up your ball and moving on.
- *"That's good"* has nothing to do with your form. An opponent will call this out to you when he wishes to indicate that you need not continue putting, that he will concede that you can make the next putt in one stroke, that you should add one stroke to your score from where the ball came to rest, pick it up, and be on your way.
- *"We're playing two, two, and two."* It would take a book to describe all the variables of Nassau wagering. But what has been indicated to you here is that there is probably a two dollar

bet on the front nine holes, a two dollar bet on the second nine holes, and a two dollar bet for the 18 holes. You just may wish to clarify that two means two dollars and not two hundred. Some pretty good sticks often play for a nickel, but they can mean five dollars or five hundred.

• *"We're playing them down"* means that you are truly going to play the game as it was designed to be played, under USGA Rules and Regulations. You play the ball wherever it is. In a divot, you don't move it out. Behind a tree, you either knock it out or take a penalty drop. The opposite variation of this is called "winter rules." Pretty much a disgrace to golf, for serious golfers, unless professionals or officials have decided that your course is literally unplayable due to heavy rains or other conditions.

We can't nudge the ball up onto a tuft of grass because even the slightest nudge costs a stroke. Far worse, the nudger will be thought of as a cheat. Serious golfers are quite tolerant of dummies, but there's absolutely no tolerance for cheaters. Intentional cheaters will never get another game with most golfers.

As you know, *you* are the referee when it comes to calling a violation on yourself. And that is the proper procedure; announcing immediately to the other players for instance, "I double hit that pitch shot for a cost of two strokes." (Imagine a football player saying to the ref, "I'm afraid I should tell you I was two inches off-side on that play and I suggest you penalize my team five yards.")

To understand golf is to understand self-discipline. It's a rugged individualistic game. You can't expect teammates or "zebras" to catch your rule infraction. You are your opponent. Not the weather, the course, or other players. It's you conquering yourself in shot making and behavior and that's why, to many of us, golf is the ultimate contest.

Perhaps the most delicate of situations is suggesting or calling out a rule infraction made by one of your players. First, be very sure you're right. Then call it gently. The most common mistake is miscounting the number of strokes taken. You could say, "Joe, I wonder if you'd mind recounting your strokes. It seems to me you forgot one or two."

Or, "Friend Joe, I know it was hard for you to see but I do believe your club touched the sand on your backswing." (A penalty of two strokes in Stroke Play, loss of hole in Match Play.) When there is a rules dispute on a hole, the player involved should play a second provisional ball, then check with the pro in the golf shop for accurate answers.

Let's talk further about golf vocabulary. I realize some terms are indigenous to the West Coast—others as passe or vernacular as "boss" or "bitchin," but some hang in there.

- *"What are you?"* The answer is not Republican or Democrat. The question asks how many strokes are you thus far on that hole.
- *"You hit it stiff."* You've hit the ball exactly the right distance to the hole. You're "hole high."
- *"Whatdja shoot?"* "The highway" (that means 101). "The strip" (that means 77, as in Sunset Strip). "Trombones" (that's 76 as in . . .).
- *"I hit a cowboy."* It was a drifter, left to right.
- *"Army style."* Left, right, left, right.
- One that has always intrigued me that I've found very prevalent with the big boy pros (tour)—*"What did you have on three?"* *"I make four."* Now, why not "I *made* four?" Don't ask me. I don't know.
- But here's something more important to you. You don't *shoot* golf. You play golf, and the score is what you shoot. *"Oh, I'm going out to shoot golf."* The experienced golfer says to himself, "We have just heard from a nincompoop."
- *"Chili dip."* You hit behind it and it moved only a couple of feet. Kerplunk.
- *"Skulled it."* Hit the top part of the ball, topping it—a dub.
- *"Shanked."* It squirted off right, hit more on the hosel of the shaft than the face of the club. (See a psychiatrist.)

- *"Burned it."* A putt came *very* close to falling after traveling over the lip of the cup.
- *"Bite."* The backspin one often desires—wanting the ball to stop or back up.

A quick note. When you've putted your ball into the hole (holed out), don't leave it in there. Reach in and pick it out. Old superstition says two balls cannot get in the hole. Get it out and move to the next tee.

The lexicon of golf is almost endless. The vocal demonstrations are something else. I can remember playing one time in a small tournament at Skyline, in Arizona, courtesy of Bud Gravette, a long-time close friend. Big man in finance. Big man in better golfing circles. Anyway, I had "drawn" a huge man for a partner. An oil "bidnez" guy. Paunch. Cigar. Balding. Suspicious of my capabilities. Used to being boss. He said on the tee, "You hit first!" I did. And it was one of those career drives that was long and perfect. Oil Bidnez jumped up on the tee and yelled with a wild, squatting, pointing gesture down the fairway, "Son, you have heet it farther than I can see and straighter than I kin pint!"

Then there's mumbler vocabulary. The late Dick Grout, dear friend and senior PGA pro, used to console himself after a bad shot by muttering, "The cuddy roons aroun' the braize. He shytes amongst the neighbors claithes. The more you shoo the more he shytes, aye what a vulger bugger he is." That took up some time as he ambled to his next shot. Loosely translated, this Scotch ditty has to do with a jackass distributing his leavings all over freshly washed clothes laid out in a pasture to dry.

Dick was a story-telling legend, brother of teacher Jack Grout of Nicklaus fame. He was a winner of many tournaments back when he and his wife would take off with Ben Hogan and his wife, and flip to see who rode in the open rumble seat to the next tourney that maybe paid the winner a couple of hundred dollars.

So much for getting ready. You now know where you're going, been refreshed or introduced to some of the vernacular, and know how to look the part. What you've done is gotten yourself ready to enjoy the game and prepared yourself for others to enjoy you.

Oh, one other thing. It's about the word "fore." It means duck. Hold your head. Get the hell out of the way. There is a golf ball coming at you that is just as lethal as a Civil War cannonball. If this word is shouted in your direction, take what cover you can. The game can be damnably dangerous. Is this just a whole lot of fun so far? It'll get better, and easier.

The Arrival
at the Club

L et's presume we're headed for a private club. We're about to
announce ourselves. We are about to drive or have just driven onto the premises of the country club. We may well be
greeted by a guard. It'll probably look like we need a ticket to
get in. We announce our names to the guard and whose guest
we are to be that day. He or she will have done their duty by in-
forming the guard of our expected arrival. If we neglected to ask
where we drop our bags in a waiting rack for pick-up, this is our
opportunity to ask. We proceed to that area and the parking area
closest to that. We park the car. Remove our equipment from
the trunk, which would also include shoe bags for our golf shoes
and perhaps dining room attire for later, if that's the game plan.
Our next stop is the golf shop. Anyone will be delighted to guide
us there. Public or private, the golf shop is the first stop.

At the private club, we will then announce to the pro or one
of his assistants our name and the member's name who is host-
ing us, and that we wish to inform him that we are on the
premises. We will be thanked and probably advised as to
whether our host has yet arrived. At the public course, it's at the
golf shop we pay our green fee and cart, or trolley, fee and are
directed usually to a Starter for a tee time.

Having announced ourselves to the pro, we take advantage
of this opportunity to request a scorecard. In the next few
minutes we'll have an opportunity to review at least the first
hole. Why? This will tell us in advance the yardage and what is

par for the hole, and thus will suggest to us what club we will probably use for our first shot on the Number One tee. An iron? A driver? Later we'll get a hint as to what is probably best by following the lead of the other players of our foursome. But at least we'll be knowledgeable enough to know whether we're facing a three par, four par, or a five par and, if the scorecard contains some sort of a diagram of the holes, what we can expect on Number One.

This will also give us an opportunity, prior to facing the course, to read the scorecard's *Local Rules*. Each course may have a few *Local Rules* that supplant or make clearer its interpretation of the United States Golf Association (USGA) rules. For instance: "Ball coming to rest in a flower bed so marked by blue stakes may be dropped one club length at the nearest point of relief no nearer the hole, no penalty." "The water on Number Four is to be played as a lateral hazard." Meaning among other alternatives, a player can drop at the closest spot where the ball entered the water for a penalty of one stroke, as opposed to a lost ball, two-stroke penalty.

At the private club, we ask at the golf shop how we proceed to the locker room. Upon arriving at the locker room, seek out the locker room attendant. Again we announce our names and the member host's name. The attendant will then make one of two decisions, depending on club facilities and rules.

We will either be assigned a locker near that of our host, or the locker room attendant may elect to have us share our host's locker. In either event, he will direct us to, and open, a locker for us. We'll ask him, "Should we put our spikes (golf shoes) on now? Are they permissible in the Grill?" We will probably be advised that golf shoes are permitted in the Grill, and he will point the way. It may well be that that's where our host intends to meet us.

Having geared ourselves for golf, we proceed to the Grill. (We haven't tipped the locker man; it's not time yet.) If we did, however, leave our dress shoes in front of our locker, we've indicated that we would appreciate their being shined. The locker room attendant will collect them, shine them, and have them prepared for us to pick up after our game. Needed or not, leaving our dress shoes or sports shoes for a shine is a common practice.

At any golf course the "assembly room" is usually the Grill. At the private club, the waiter approaches us, we again identify ourselves and the name of our host, and we will either be directed to our host's table or an empty table to await his arrival. We'll probably be asked if we would like coffee, tea, or a drink. Remember, at the private club we're ordinarily encountering a no-cash-accepted situation. So we don't offer to pay.

We merely receive the check and let it sit by our drink until our host arrives. He or she may have gotten held up and could be a little late. However, the host should have made every endeavor to be at the club *before* you arrive. If the waiter asks if we care for anything else, the answer is no; we will await our host or hostess.

If they're not there already, they'll be filtering in, and the waiter or captain, having been alerted, will direct the remainder of our group to us at the table.

Beware of wearing a hat inside. It's a sure tip-off of "bumpkin." Not executive at all!

Hubie Hatrack says, "But I thought we were just a bunch of the guys hanging out." No way. Business associates may wonder if that might be his style at the office. Hats indoors are teeny-bopper stuff, where kids wore their caps after Little League and headed for the pizza parlor.

We know, of course, that it's really not a good idea to ever wear a hat that says Tiger Claw Tires, Fergy's Fertilizer, or the like. The only safe hat has a club emblem on it or some such symbol that does not suggest a walking billboard. Some tour players get paid to wear logos on their hats, but they are pros, and rely on endorsement money for income as well. The bottom line is, when under a ceiling, the hat is off. It's not only off, it is on a hat rack or on the floor underneath the chair. It certainly is never on top of the table where the perspiration band reinforces one's presence.

Hubie Hatrack

The Grill is social time. There'll be friendly arguments as to who are to be partners—will it be the highest handicap coupled with the lowest handicap? Some such system will evolve, or a couple of players will challenge the other two.

The good-natured lying usually starts in the Grill. After listening to years upon years of pre-game conversation, I would say the following comments about cover the range of subjects:

• "I'm still suffering from jet lag. I didn't get in from London until two o'clock this morning." This and those to follow will only indicate, "Please have sympathy for me and my poor game."

• "I can actually play much better. I just never have." (My favorite!)

• "I was up practically all night. I think we got home from that Charity Event at 3 A.M."

• "I don't know whether to have another shot of cortisone for this elbow or not."

- "My back just doesn't seem to get any better. It goes out more than I do. I don't know why I'm playing."
- "Well, it's been nine weeks now since I've played. I'll be a basket case."
- "Oh I wish I could have had you guys two weeks ago. I burned it up with an 83. Last time out, 95."
- "I just got these new clubs. Have no idea how they'll work."
- "I had a lesson the other day. So you know I'm going to be paralyzed."
- "I can't play in weather like this."
- "It's so hard to concentrate when you have so many business problems."
- "There's never any time for me to practice, I'm so busy all the time."
- "I'm going to lay off for six months, and then I intend to quit."
- "Yeah, I play once a year just to stay sharp."

And *you* feel nervous or intimidated? There are variations on this theme, but each player feels bound and determined that if it were not for one thing or another, surely he would be on tour.

Anyway, they will probably recount to us previous days of glory and previous days of disaster. All good-natured fun preceding the entourage's entry onto the executive proving grounds.

If there's time, there may be a light bite to eat and perhaps a visit to the driving range to warm up and hit a few balls. There probably won't be time enough to consider it a practice session, and indeed it shouldn't be. But if we are offered the opportunity, we will accept it, for it holds forth advantages. If you sting your hands on a couple of shots at the range, you're going to be more fit and ready for the first tee. And, moreover, a few good wallops along with a few short shots will help release any tension that has been building up. The drill at the practice range will probably consist of hitting a small bucket of balls. Good players, as well as the medical profession, recommend that we hit a few short shots to limber up, then move on up to a few drives to conclude, so that our muscles are a bit more supple on the tee, less susceptible to muscle strains or cramps.

The practice tee story that I feel is most recountable is the one about the golfer who, after completing a practice session, rushes up to a group of his friends with tremendous exuberance and exclaims, *"I've found it! I know the secret of golf! There is no doubt about it! It's infallible! It's absolute! I'm sure of it!* (Pause.) *And if that doesn't work, I've got another idea."*

It is now *de rigueur* to head for the putting green. After all, we have to get a feel for these greens, right? Are they coarse? Are they long? Are they fast? Is there a great deal of undulation? The putting green should give us a number of clues as to what to expect of the greens out on the course. There should be great similarity. Let's get the feel for the long putts first. How hard do we have to hit to go from here to there. Finish up with a couple of 3-foot tap-ins, and we're ready.

Head for the first tee and "let the games commence."

The First
Tee: Hole
Number One

I f balls are to be thrown in the air to determine partners (the closest two balls becoming partners), we'll announce to the thrower the make and number of the ball that each of us is handing him. If some other player is playing the identical ball, we'll offer to switch in order to avoid confusion. Or we will identify your ball with some mark from a marking pen.

While all of this is taking place, you may feel a sudden urge to take just a few more practice swings. Get totally away from people if you wish to do this. Also, make sure you're not setting up to take a practice swing if someone else is in the actual act of hitting his shot.

And never take a practice swing here or anywhere on the course toward anyone who is nearby. You might swing down and take a bite of turf that could fly out and blind someone.

On the tee, each of us will want to be sure that we have four major ingredients in our pockets and that's all, other than perhaps a billfold and handkerchief. The first of four necessities is a couple of balls. They can be of the same make but must have different numerals or markings to distinguish them apart. Second are a few tees. Third, we'll need a divot repair tool. This is a small hand-held pronged device to repair indented turf. Then we are quite ready to repair ball marks that our ball has left on the greens, those pock-marked indications where our ball has landed. Finally, we'll want a few ball markers, small circular plastic chips to mark our ball's placement on the green.

At least one major ingredient that does *not* belong in the pocket is car keys, which may rattle incessantly at just the wrong time and distract players with their annoying jingling noise.

We do know, of course, that we stand still and maintain absolute silence whenever another player is striking the ball.

Let's note that there are different colored tee markers—the place from which we start. These may be the farthest back championship tees, intermediate tees, or front tees. We may even be asked which set of tees we prefer. Our answer is, "Whatever you gentlemen prefer." Our day will come for determining whether we want to take on the whole monster and see the entire course or play the short yardage variety.

The next question is who hits first? This is not an arbitrary decision. A flip of a tee thrown in the air may come down and point to you. In which case, it would mean that your team would occupy the tee first. *Your honors.*

If we have a host, he will likely indicate with a gesture to one of us, "Let our guests go first."

Professionals will and can advise you on what a lot of people say is the most difficult shot in golf, the first shot. From my own experience, I merely try to think of an unhurried swing and of not trying to knock the cover off it with the first swing. Some little voice inside of you says, "Show 'em how strong you are. Knock the 'doglogs' out of it." Don't listen. It's Satan talking.

If it is any consolation to you, I can remember playing one time in a national amateur event that attracted a huge gallery. I stood over the ball. Was aware of galleries both left and right. And quietly but fervently implored the Lord, "God, I don't care where it goes. Just please let me make contact." And I did!

The first shot is somewhat like making your first solo flight. The odds are all in favor of your performing far better than you could have possibly hoped. And I expect that's what will happen with you. But, just in case it trickles off there at 20 or 30 yards, and even though your friends may suggest it, never let the idea of a *mulligan* come to mind. A mulligan is an extra free stroke.

Illegal! It's also referred to as a "breakfast ball." "Hit 'til you *like* it." All, in general, mean, "Oh, what the hell, let's break the rules already and hit another one and not count the first one." Decline. Best you should say with a smile, "I put it there. I'll hit it from there." You will have made your first big impression. You go by the book. You accept your fate without complaint. You accept the consequences without alibis. You've taken that first giant step toward proper golf etiquette.

But what if it goes out-of-bounds? Now you're obligated to hit another ball and wherever it lands (presuming the first ball is out of bounds) you will lie three including your two penalty strokes (stroke and distance). But before you strike that second ball, *always* make an announcement. You announce the make and number of your first ball and then the make and number of your second ball. This is saying, in effect, I certainly will not try to incorrectly claim the ball that is *in* bounds as being my first. Your statement goes something like this, "My first ball was a Titleist #1. And this is a Titleist #3." Don't carry two balls of identical make and number in your pocket.

Proper Observation Position

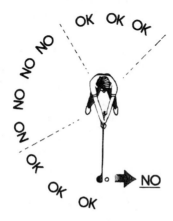

Now, step away after retrieving your tee. The reason you don't leave the tee is that it will foul up the grass mowers. Pick it up, repocket it, move outside the teeing area, and face the player who is hitting. Do not get directly in back of him. Surely not in front of him. You want to be right across from him, off about seven yards, so that if he were to tilt his head up at address he can see you. Reason? So he's sure he's not going to bop you on the head with a backswing or follow through. This holds true, by the way, throughout the course. We never get directly in back of the player's ball. We don't put our cart directly behind a player. We keep in his view by either squarely facing him or by being slightly to the rear, so that if he squirts a shot off oblique right or left it will not konk us on the head.

It is not only golf that is a four-letter word. You shouldn't be a bit surprised to hear some other language on that first tee or very shortly thereafter. Even with old hands, there's a bit of tension relief having completed this first stroke, and sometimes the comments are directed to the ball—which has just become a mortal enemy. "Don't go there, you . . . stop . . . go . . . not in the sand, you . . . ," etc.

Proceeding to the nearest ball on the fairway, there'll probably be some reconfirmation of the bets, and if we don't understand them, we'll ask. But quite quickly now, see if you can spot where your ball came to rest in relationship to the 150-yard markers. It's quite proper if you're confused about distance, and if you're riding with your partner, to ask the approximate yardage to the green.

As an aside, there are some flag position indications that can help you. Remember that indicated yardages are to the *center* of the green. Let's say the flag (pin) is on the *front* of the green. Sometimes a ball attached to the flagpole gives us information. Ball low means the hole is located on the front of the green; high, the back of the green. What's becoming more popular are three colors of flags. Red, up front (just like the teeing location); white, in the middle (like the middle tees); and blue, the hole is located far back (as are the blue tees).

Before you get to your ball, you're already figuring out your game plan for stroke Number Two. Do you go for it? Do you lay it up? You know the object. Hit the ball in the hole with the fewest number of strokes. How could you best do that, short of a miracle? That's your solution: the one that's short of a miracle. Especially early in the round, don't place too big a burden on yourself for *par excellence.*

As mentioned earlier, one does not have to be a golf master to determine who is farthest away from the hole, presuming one can see where he is, where others are, and the location of the flagstick on the green. But if you can't, feel free to confirm with your partner, "It appears I'm away, would you agree?" Then proceed.

Let's presume, that you are not the farthest one away from the pin, and that you want to take a few practice strokes. Definitely do not face the hole and take your stance at your ball, even if you're a foot or two away from the ball, and direct your practice swings *toward the green.* The reason is simply that another player may presume that you have determined that you are the farthest out and that you are preparing to hit. His courtesy to you will be to wait until you've finished, thus delaying the game. If there is a lag time between shots, and you want to take a few practice swings, that's fine, but turn away from the green so there's no doubt in anyone's mind that you're not preparing to strike the ball.

♀ Oh, you say, there are so many things to remember. True. But take heart. No one is ever able, at all times, to keep all of these etiquette tips in mind. None of us is perfect. The sole intent is to improve one's golf manners and make the game more fun for all. If you are a beginner, the experienced and serious golfers you may play with have all been where you are now. You'll find understanding and great empathy, an eagerness to assist you when you show any evidence of trying to help yourself along the way.

And remember, our objective is to create the right image for you—the net impression of a person intent on improvement, with a positive, pleasant attitude.

At last the players have arrived "on the dance floor": All the balls are on the green. The first move is for all players to place a ball mark directly *behind* their ball. Each is then allowed to pick up his ball and clean it at this time, and this is a good idea. A clean ball putts truer. The only player to immediately place his ball back into position, just ahead of his marker, is the player farthest away from the hole. The player farthest away putts first. If you were to have a caddie, and your ball was the first ball on the green, it would be his responsibility to tend the flag. Without a caddie, it's the responsibility of the closest player to the hole to tend the flagstick.

Let's presume that's you. Call out the player's name that you think is farthest from the hole indicating it's his putt. "John, I believe you're away. Would you like the flag tended or removed?" If he would prefer it tended, grab the flag attached to the flagpole (so it won't flap about), and hold it to the flagpole keeping the pin in the hole. Be very careful in holding the pin that your feet are not stepping on the line of another players putt, that is on the grass someplace between his ball and the cup. Otherwise his ball may have to be putted over this indentation and could jump off track like a grasshopper. Also, we must always be aware that our shadow does not fall across a players line or the cup itself. As the player strikes his putt, remove the flagstick and step aside.

A person once inquired, "On which side of the hole should you stand to hold the flagstick, presuming you will not be standing in any player's line of putt?" The answer is, the *high* side of the hole. It's referred to as the "nice guy" side or the "pro side." In other words, your feet may be a nice target for the next putter, because by standing on the high side, the ball aimed there, would probably break toward the hole from your feet. It's no big deal. But it's the nice way and shows a touch of class.

Now ask, "Can everyone else see it all right?" If they can, take the flag over to the *fringe* of the green and place it down there on the ground. The *fringe* is that small, circular area of grass between the actual green and the fairway. If you must place it on the green, place it out of the way of everyone. We know to lay it down gently. Do not toss it.

Keep in mind, in this scenario, since you were the closest, your very first obligation, even before tending the flag, was to place a ball marker directly behind your ball—not to the side and not in front, but directly behind. Other players, other than the one farthest away will have immediately done the same thing.

What is used for a marker should be given some consideration. A penny is frowned upon, because it's too difficult for opposing players to see, and thus they might inadvertently walk in that player's line of putt. A quarter, half dollar, tee, or divot tool won't do because that will obstruct the roll of someone else's ball. The big boys on the tour all seem to favor marking with a dime. Why? Don't ask. I don't know. But there are ball markers made for just this sort of thing that are available from the pro shop.

This whole business of how to mark and where to stand on the green is vitally important, and I can't emphasize it too much. In the beginning I always felt like a very awkward hopscotch player, but soon proper actions became second nature.

Where do we position ourselves while others are putting? We do not stand directly behind the person putting so that he can see us with peripheral vision. We have two places to stand. Stand where we're facing his back, or stand opposite of him where we are somewhat facing him.

The whole point is that he should see nothing in his vision in back of him and nothing in front of him except the hole. As soon as his putter has struck the ball and just as soon as his ball has come to rest, he has an immediate obligation. He doesn't just stand there and stare, or lament the fact that it's five feet short or five feet long. He immediately signals his intent.

He says one of two things. "I'll mark that ball," at which point he moves forward in a manner not to step on anyone's line of putt, and goes to his ball and marks it, awaiting his next turn. His other elective in a "friendly" match is to say, "I wish to finish it out." Whereupon he goes to his ball and does indeed attempt to finish out—complete the hole. But these are the only two prerogatives. You mark it or putt it. There's no in between. No matter where it came to rest, history somehow bears out, staring at it will not cause it to move—especially toward the hole.

Another situation may arise that you should know about. Let's presume that you have marked your ball. And that your dime or ball marker is placed on a line that would deflect another putt or disturb a golfer who would be putting directly over that line. He may say to you, "Please mark your ball one to the left or one to the right." If he does, then go to your marker. Place your putter head one length to the left or right, lining the club head up with a tree or some permanent object. Then place your marker down in front of the tip of the putter. If he calls for you to move it two, then you would take it two putter heads right or left.

Remember, when it is your turn to putt, move your marker back in the identical manner in which you moved it away at his request. Then place your ball in front of that original marker. Otherwise a two-stroke penalty occurs against you.

Hole Number One has been a tough one, with lots to remember. Hopefully, during some practice round beforehand, you've had an opportunity to get most of these details mentally in order. In any event, the *moment* you have holed out your ball, that is *finished,* or been conceded a *gimme,* call out your score. That was a five, or that was a three, or that was a seven. But say it loudly enough to be heard so that the general score-keeper doesn't have to ask eighteen times a day, "Hey, what'd you have?" More on this later. Don't figure "net." Figure "gross." The master scorekeeper will figure your net. He'll probably announce the results of the first hole while we're on the second tee.

A couple of other pointers before we get to the second tee. Perhaps you've seen the very tricky maneuver of someone not picking his ball out of the hole but rather placing his clubhead putter into the hole and flipping the ball out. No good. The shaft of his putter will undoubtedly break down the lip of the cup. And as tricky as it looks, or as clever as it may be, it's the sign of a dumb wise guy.

Also, before getting to the second tee let's review your own particular style of scoring. It has been my experience that it is virtually impossible for anyone to keep his or her score by counting back-wards. Something like, to oneself, "Let's see, I had two putts on the green, before that I was back over there, around the trap, that would be three, before that I was back there by that grass bunker— that's four, then I was at about the 150 mark—that was five . . ."

No! Won't work! One cannot count backwards accurately. What you should do is silently keep track of your strokes as you *proceed* on the hole. You silently say, that's one. And now I lay two, and now three. And you know where you are at all times by counting forward, never backward. There are also a couple of words that have no place in the proper golf vocabulary. They are as follows: I had *about* a seven. I had *like* a six. There are no "about's" and there are no "like's." Scores are called out precisely. You had what you had and an approximation won't get the job done. If you're new, and don't know whether a penalty is a one stroke or a two stroke, consult your playing partner at that time so that you'll know your stroke count before taking your next swing. If the chairman or C.E.O. were to ask someone what interest was being paid on a short-term debt, and the person in charge of same answered "approximately" or "about a," that wouldn't get the job done, would it?

On the way over to the second hole, let's take this opportunity to look at the yardage of the hole and what the par figure is for it. Let's try to get a few fundamentals straight in our mind before reaching the tee.

A couple of different alternatives may happen on this tee. The host may announce that we will play by the *honor system,* meaning that the team that won the last hole will tee off first. Of that team, you may be the lead man on the front nine and your partner, the lead man of the second nine holes. Or, your host or a chorus may announce, "We hit when ready." It means just that. The honor system is abandoned and, perhaps to speed up play, one should strike it when ready. However, my best advice to you if you are a newcomer would be to hit last. It gives you more thinking time for one thing. And, second, you get to hear the ooh's and ah's for a good shot preceding you, depending on where it landed, and the moans and groans of a shot indicating where you don't want to go.

In any event, prepare yourself totally with ball, tee, and club, standing on the tee facing the player who is now swinging, or slightly to the rear so that when it is your turn, there's no delay. If you feel like taking a practice swing, wait until you've teed your ball, be a foot or two away from it, take your practice swing, which is fine, step up to it, and give it a belt.

There is a slight possibility that right about now you may feel browbeaten by all of these details. So we're going to magically remove you now from this foursome as we move on into the next few chapters. There you and I will hover about and watch other players along the way that consciously or unconsciously are ruining their image while obliterating their chances of winning friends or business success.

Though they have various nicknames, they are the "Bob Bunglers" of golf, the ones sure to pay attention when someone yells, "Hey, dummy!"

Here Come
the Bunglers

"If there's any dog in ya, golf will bring it out."

Today may very well be Guest Day at Rich Land Country Club and you are there. By special powers endowed to us by the Golf Gods, we are going to travel the course and take a peek at a lot of people who are having some monstrous moments.

We'll visit foursomes around the course. These foursomes are made up of various players. A variety of "Bob Bunglers" are among the foursomes. The Bunglers have made no preparation in learning the manners of the game, so look out, here they come.

I've asked our Pro of Protocol to join us. He comments on the rights and wrongs, and he speaks in a foreign tongue: *Italics*. Now the Tour de Course.

Dicky Divotdigger

♀ PRO of PROTOCOL: *"Note that it's perfectly all right that Dicky Boy takes a fairway divot, that clump of dirt and grass that snaps into the air as a club smacks into a ball. He can have at it like a ditchdigger, if that's his style. The point is, at the completion of his shot, it is his responsibility to make sure that the divot is replaced. When is a divot replaceable? Look at the spot where the ball was lying. Would you like your ball to come to rest in that very same spot? If not, then the divot should be repaired."*

Dicky Divotdigger

That's hitting it down the old pipeline.

In most areas of the country, if turf has been cut out that has exposed roots and is quickly replaced, the grass should regrow. There are certain courses where they prefer that the divot be replaced with sand from a little sandbucket to be found on the cart.

Other courses, many of them in Asia, practice filling the divot immediately with a mixture of dirt and seed smoothed over by a caddie with the deftness of a plastic surgeon. It only takes a moment to fill, stomp, and move on.

The other type of divot in golf is actually a ballmark on the green. You'll notice that when Dicky's ball landed on the green it made an indentation. Expert green superintendents tell us that if this is repaired immediately, it will heal in just a few hours, while if it's left untended, it takes literally days before the green heals itself. In the meantime, somebody's putt hits the indentation (the ballmark), the ball goes awry and it wasn't really a bad break at all. It was bad deportment by the player who left the indentation.

In short: Show me a golfer who does not carry a divot repair tool for the green and I'll show you a "Bob Bungler."

The other players may be silently musing: "Well, if he doesn't make it as a V.P., I guess I know where the next ditchdigger is coming from."

"His attention to detail is a wee bit lacking."

"He's confused. That's the kind of competitor I like to be up against."

His image is being damaged badly.

Sylvester Standbad

I gotta feeling this is going to be a real cruncher.

Sylvester Standbad

⚲ PRO of PROTOCOL: *"Look at where poor old Sylvester is standing. He's too close, and he's directly behind the player that's now playing the shot. He's forgotten to refer to that figure on page 43 of where one stands when another player is hitting. This is not merely a matter of etiquette. He's walked into a danger zone directly behind and close, whereby he could be inadvertently struck by that player."*

The other players wonder if Sylvester is this aimless at the office. His mind is a thousand miles away. Hopefully, he will come to his senses before getting to the green. If he stands directly behind someone who is putting, or directly in his vision as he faces the hole, he'll be asked to move either left or right. Another blow to his image.

Harry Huntsman

The Great White Hunter . . . or was it Orange?
Maybe Optic Yellow?

Harry Huntsman

♀ PRO of PROTOCOL: *"Well, the five-minute legal time limit to look for the ball has gone the way of the broken watch. He should give up. I hope he then remembers that he doesn't just drop one, but that he goes back to where he hit it from originally, taking a two-shot, lost ball penalty. Stroke and distance."*

Others in his group wonder:
"What a sense of timing! I wonder if he wastes time like this at the office. The ball only costs a couple of bucks. I wonder if he spends that much valuable time looking for a lost pencil at the office."
"Is he pennywise, pound foolish?"
"This is not an Easter egg hunt. Why doesn't he get on about the business of playing golf?"
The image crisis is just that, a crisis.

Sammy Sahara

You guys play through. I am going to play until I am through.

Sammy Sahara

♀ PRO OF PROTOCOL: *"Sammy Sahara's attitude is preferable to the player who becomes furious at landing in a bunker. When one is playing the sand shot, if the player's clubhead touches the sand at address or on the way back, there is a penalty. Practice your sand shot address by keeping your club a couple of inches above the sand. That business of just 1/16 inch above the sand is going to cost sooner or later. It's just a hazard. Nothing terminal. "*

Sammy's situation has several do's and don'ts. First of all, a player should walk into the trap and out of the trap in the same footsteps. That way there's only one area to rake. Rakes belong where they least affect play. Normally, in the trap, not out and about. And they should be parallel with the fairway. At some courses in Florida, we'll also find canisters that are used as rake holders. If one had to blast out of the sand and thus splashed a whole dune of sand on the green, the flat part of the rake is to pull the sand back into the trap. We must leave the trap as we found it. You say your ball came to rest in somebody else's heavy footprint. Well, that's called "rub of the green." Don't ask me why. I don't know. It has nothing whatsoever to do with the green. What it *does* have to do with is that you must play the ball as you found it, and that includes when it comes to rest on the top of leaves, a branch, or the totally buried fender from a Hudson automobile.

Tiptoe Thompson

♀ PRO of PROTOCOL: *"Here's old 260-pound Tippy. He's right out of the Heavystepper stable. He evidently is not deft enough to step around the line of a putt, and somehow seems to think that if he were to tip-toe right on top of the line of a putt this would either not matter, or be quickly forgiven. Great for toe dancers. Lousy for serious golfers."*

We've got to look where we're going before we go. An old explanation goes like this. "Oh, there were a thousand feet there before, a couple more won't make the difference." Wrong.

From the time the last golfer was there, that grass has had a chance to re-elevate itself, to spring back into place.

Yes, it takes a few minutes, but if we're putting before these few minutes have elapsed, that little white ball is going to run right over a grass barricade, flipping left or right and, probably, not the direction we want.

Tippy in his heartfelt, clumsy sympathy says, "I'm sorry about that. Take that putt over." And if the putter so elects, both are penalized. There is no nice solution to this problem.

And his business group contemplates:

"I can just see this guy tip-toeing into a board room. First into the potted plant, rebounding into the person having a sip of coffee, then using his necktie to wipe up the mess before falling over in somebody else's chair. He's a hell of a dancer!"

It's time for some repast.

Tiptoe Thompson

Me. I'm always careful so's to leave a good impression

THE HALFWAY HOUSE

Why do they call it the Halfway House? Some suspect it's because its placed at a spot where one is halfway done playing golf. Where you've completed nine holes. Quite the opposite of professionals, it is customary that amateur foursomes stop at the Halfway House for a variety of reasons.

Usually there are bathrooms here as well as a couple of other locations on the course. There is a chance to assemble the group in some proximity and explain why your first nine holes were merely a warm-up session and that surely you'll shoot the course record on the second nine. It is a time when the master scorekeeper will probably advise us of our financial gambling status with the other players. Just an, "Oh, I see," will usually suffice at this point, rather than, "You rotten sombitch, I'll bury you on the backside."

It's ha, ha, ha and we'll all do better on the back nine. It's also time for a beer or a soft drink and perhaps even a snack. On many courses, there's a phone-in system to the Halfway House on Hole Number Eight, whereby those players who want hot sandwiches can phone them in and have them put on the grill, so they'll be ready upon arrival.

Again, at the private club, the strongest likelihood is that cash is not accepted. Our host will undoubtedly sign for whatever refreshments we have ordered or he may engage in a bit of dice rolling with the other members to see who picks up the tab. In any event, guests are treated.

We may find that this is the spot where a member or a regular player of the course will ask what we think of the course. I'm reminded of what young pros are told when they are attending PGA School prior to the tour. They're cautioned that this question may come up. Their reply paraphrases this thought: "This is the best course, *of its type,* I have ever played." If the members of a private layout didn't think this was the best, they probably wouldn't be members. So comments like, "The greens are uneven. The sand has different consistencies. Did Ray Charles lay this thing out? Don't they ever mow the fairways? They oughta hold safaris in these roughs. Who can play on this billygoat hill," etc. just won't make it.

As a matter of fact, if it is a private club, it probably receives much lighter play than any public course. So the condition of the golf course will most likely be manicured to a fare-thee-well and maintained immaculately . . . at least by comparison.

Normally there's a telephone at the halfway point, and if you need to make a call at a private club, ask your host how to get the operator or an outside line. Sometimes local calls are gratis. Sometimes there are charges to the member host's club number, and there is often a combination by which you can go through the club operator with a credit card call and avoid any confusion whatsoever about charges.

A group will not tarry long for fear of holding up foursomes coming behind.

So someone will probably say, "Onward and upward. Let's have at it for the back nine." Many Halfway Houses do not have bussing staff. It's a good idea for us to keep alert and if our fellow golfers are policing their table, depositing their litter, that's a clue that we should do the same.

Someone is bound to make you feel better at this point with the inevitable comment, "Now we come to the *tough* part of the golf course." It may or may not be true. He's merely testing your

Do not be a Rolly Rollflasher.

blood pressure. Good. You love a challenge. A walk in the park. A day to be remembered. And while all of this was going on, it would have been very wise of you to sneak another glance at the scorecard, so that you can determine the yardage of Number 10, as well as the par figure. If the desirable target is obscured, it's perfect protocol to ask your partner, "If I'm lucky enough, where is the best target for my first shot?"

FOLLOW THE SIGNS

Most good golf clubs try to hold signage to a minimum. Rightly so. However: When you see a sign that says "SCATTER" it means, *don't* follow the leader with your cart so the grass won't mat down to dirt or mud because of repeated traction.

ARROWS guide you on the correct route carts should take.

WHITE painted enclosures on the grass indicate that the enclosed area is "ground under repair"—and if your ball comes to rest on or within the stripe, or if when you take your stance to address your ball your feet touch the stripe or are within the enclosure, you may drop your ball away from the area to the nearest area of relief, no closer to the hole without penalty.

WAVE WAITING PLAYERS ON: When playing a par 3 and all of your group have arrived at the green, wave other waiting players on the tee to go ahead and hit their tee shots (and watch so as to not get hit before you start putting).

WHITE STAKES are a sign of out-of-bounds. If your ball comes to rest outside the line between two white stakes you are out of bounds. The shot must be replayed from *where you were standing* when the ball was hit out of bounds. Any part of the ball on the boundary line is considered in bounds.

The 90° sign means keep your cart on the cart path until you come to the ball next in play. Then turn your cart 90 degrees to go to the ball for club selection and play—and then 90 degrees right back to the cart path.

CARTS MUST STAY ON PATHS AT ALL TIMES.

Inconvenient, but those are the rules.

Let's get back to our bunglers.

Peter Pinjabber

♀ PRO of PROTOCOL: *"When taking the pin out for one putter and awaiting the instructions of the next, Peter should hold the flag horizontally, out of the line of sight. If he allows the butt of it to jab into the green, he has thoughtlessly created another one of those indentations that we're trying to eliminate."*

And some corporate members in Peter Pinjabber's group wonder, "Is this the way he would treat a company car?"

Peter also has another beauty habit. He leans heavily on his putter like a cane, creating a deep crease in the green in order to steady and balance himself while reaching over to retrieve the ball from the hole. Yes, he got the ball. But if that crease deflects someone's putt, his career has crashed as a result of the *Peter Principle.*

Peter Pinjabber

Yeah, well, somebody told me to take it and stick it!

Ivan Ironlitter

♀ PRO of PROTOCOL: *"Oh, Ivan! You've booted three sacred cows all in one swell foop! You don't toss those clubs you've finished using on the green. Remember what we said about those creases in the green? As those club blades hit the green, creases are made. Aside from that, now they are in the vision of the player about ready to putt. Third, as he steps backward to survey the path of his putt, he'll probably step in the middle of them, fall on his head, and spend the rest of his days suing you for concussions."*

When one has finished with the approach irons, they are to be taken over and laid on the fringe of the green until all putts are completed. Then they are retrieved, and taken to the bag. They are never to be dumped on the green.

Ivan Ironlitter

I'll leave 'em right there where we don't forget 'em, huh?

His fellow competitors wonder if ol' Ivan leaves important things scattered about his desk this way. Is he absent-minded, inconsiderate, what? The *net positive impression:* zero.

Oscar Ozone

♀ PRO of PROTOCOL: *"Oscar, at the end of every hole, the question doesn't vary a lot. It goes like this: WHAT WAS YOUR SCORE? Better yet, why should they have to ask you? Just announce it when you putt out."*

"What did you have, Oscar? And what did you have on the hole before? And the hole before that? Oscar, will you please call out your score at the end of every hole? It's bad enough I gotta keep all this mish-mash. Why do I have to ask you eighteen times what you shot? Want me to give you a signed release I'll

Oscar Ozone

This is Houston. Do you read me?
Do you read me? Over.

never tell anybody? It's bad enough I gotta add all these things up and keep track of the bloody thing."

And others might be musing about Oscar:

"I wonder if I sent him on that big deal in Cincinnati if he'd even remember to take his briefcase? I doubt if he could remember the coin he would use for a 10-cent pay toilet. *This* guy holds sales seminars?"

As the automobile man would say, "It appears Oscar is about two back of wholesale book."

Casey Clubtosser

♀ PRO of PROTOCOL: *"At any first-rate club, there will be a cease and desist of Casey. And maybe even Casey's host."*

The danger is real. (A) It might kill someone, and (B) it might deflect, rebound, and kill the tosser. It sure will cause alarm buttons to go off, like these:

"Under pressure this man can't control himself."

"He could never be boosted up the ladder to run a delicate situation in business."

"He believes that lousy shot was caused by the clubs and not himself."

"Isn't he just a little bit too old for tantrums?"

The man guilty of this gets poor grades on the scorecard of club life and needn't bother even reading the "Help Wanted" section.

He needs only to be paired with Buster Ballbanger. Then they can both be run out of business together.

Buster misses the short putt, seizes his putter handle as if it were a driver, and takes a mighty swoosh at the ball, probably removing a few inches of valuable green sod while dispensing his ball, speeding at 100 miles per hour (or more) among players in an adjoining area. Club throwing is wrong in any event, any direction. It is also a violation of protocol (not the rules) to delay the game by hitting practice putts after you have holed out.

There is only one instance of club tossing I can remember that I thought to be a comedic exception. My dear friend, Charles "Red" Scott, a big businessman, was in my foursome one day when he missed another two-foot putt. Not in anger, but in

Casey Clubtosser

*And that's how to teach a
±$★%$#! club how to behave!*

total frustration, he tossed his putter in the air directly above him, and its landing area was the top of his head.

After we had all taken out our handkerchiefs and mopped the blood from his scalp (the scalp bleeds like the devil), we moved along to the next tee. Someone finally broke the veil saying, "Red sure knocks himself out playing golf." I think it was the first and only club he has ever tossed. Anyway, it's a headache.

Beau Jingles

♀ PRO of PROTOCOL: *"Nervous! And does Beau make others nervous? Furious is a better word. He's got coins and keys that jingle, jangle, jingle. He's an in-pocket fondler. He's an unconscious mach two."*

Beau Jingles is visualized as the type who, when in a boardroom, would constantly tap his pencil and pop his chewing gum until he was suddenly popped right out of the picture. His absolute uncanny timing is to do this bit of narcissistic nonsense right when someone is bent over a short putt. You could glower at him after missing and say, "I lost my concentration." He'd be just about smart enough to go walking through a sandtrap hoping to help you find where you lost it.

Walter Whereditgo

    ♀ PRO of PROTOCOL: *"Walter, if you hadn't beat your club in the ground, hung your head in shame, crossed your eyes and otherwise gone into uncontrolled twitching you would have seen where your ball landed! "*

A player should watch where the ball goes and visually mark where it stops. Then one does not have to trouble three other people constantly saying, "Whereditgo, whereditgo?" Identify the balls location by some object near which you think it's come to rest. One shouldn't say to oneself, "over there by that tree." Which tree? Third from the end. Which end? The one with the leaves. They all have leaves. The one over there by the dog. The dog moved. The

Beau Jingles

My hitting doesn't disturb your whistling, does it?

Walter Whereditgo

It's up about another 50 yards, left or right, I'm sure. I think.

one over there where that man's lying down. Gee, I wonder if I hit him. Hope my ball didn't bounce off him into a bad lie.

Walter's group contemplates:

"If things got fast and furious at the office, I wonder if he'd always be relying on the other fellow or clerical help to bail him out from failing his own responsibilities."

Another image buster.

Mortimor Motormouth

♀ PRO of PROTOCOL: *"It's hush-a-bye baby when others are striking or preparing to strike the ball. That player probably has a human target in mind."*

Talk, talk, talk, talk. "Now let me tell you what my kids did last week and what my wife said last night at dinner. And you'll never believe what my uncle wrote me. And you know I was just thinking this very minute about what I could do given the opportunity, you understand, and if you order from me, you'll never look back and say you were sorry. And that reminds me of a little girl I met in Denver. But first I'll tell you why I sliced that ball. And why you are lunging so badly at it. But then I suspect you'd rather hear about what the guys in the men's locker have to say about that deal you pulled off a couple of weeks ago."

So long Mortimor. He's Mortimor Memoirs. *Image zapped!*

Mortimor Motormouth

We'll be right back, after this message.

The Eighteenth Hole

My friend, we have passed through many situations that have damaged many an image. You have even learned to question whether an X beats an I.P. An X on a hole means that you've totally given up and taken your ball out of play. An I.P. stands for *in pocket*. Both amount to the same thing. But now with renewed confidence, you're ready to take your last big go at it and hopefully finish up strong. I'm rootin' for you!

You know the proper order of hitting. You know which tees are being played. You know what the golf architect has designed in the way of yardage and the established par for this last hole. One of the unexplained, white-athletic-socks mysteries of golf will probably occur on the 18th tee, and that is, suddenly all matches will be contingent on the outcome of the last hole. Don't ask me why. I don't know. It just seems to happen that way. If this question has not come up before, it may come up now. Some opponent may say, "Do you wish to press?"

A *press* can be directed to you individually or to your team. In match play, it is normally acceptable to *press* when a team is two holes down. Some clubs play that when all balls are in *play*, a press occurs when a team is *three down* or *four down*— depending on the club. A *press* simply means this: *A new game is started here, while the original bets continue.* If we were betting two dollars on the side and we find ourselves two down, we can start a new bet for an equivalent amount of two dollars. It's a good way to get even. It's also a way to get deeper in debt. It all depends on your confidence, ability, and a little luck. After all, it's only money. There's an even wilder game that can sometimes come into play on the 18th tee. I don't know its origin, but I presume it comes from Hawaii. It's called "Aloha." The rough translation is, no matter how much money I'm down, it's double or nothing on this last hole. It's only money.

It's unlikely that you will finish on a hole that is a par 3. But while we're talking about gambling, let's review an extra bit of gambling that is fairly prevalent on par 3's. This is a game normally referred to as a *greenie* or a *blue plate.* Don't ask me why. I don't know.

In effect what it means is that the person who strikes the ball onto the playing surface in regulation (on a par 3, in one stroke) and is closest to the pin, and who then proceeds to two putt the hole, wins from the opposing players or teams. *Blue plates* or *greenies,* or for that matter, an up-and-down *sandy* (one stroke out of the sand, one stroke into the hole), normally are bet at 50 percent of whatever a unit is worth on a side of golf. If you're playing for two dollars a side, the *greenie* is worth a dollar.

But wait. Many club players supplement this arithmetic by adding the following caveat: If a person birdies a *greenie* or *blue plate* hole, an additional unit of one dollar is paid to the winner.

While learning all this mish-mash, you're probably better off turning to your partner and saying, "You call it, partner. I'm with you." It's only money.

The 18th hole will likely go well for you. Certainly you will be limbered up by now. Certainly you will be less intimidated. And certainly you will have achieved some confidence. Presuming you remember the previous Bungler golf situations, and then avoid them, my prediction is that you will end up a shining star.

Most golf architects design an 18th hole to really test one's mettle. Rarely is it duck soup. It can separate the strokers from the chokers. It's the finishing hole. It's the one that sends you home humming, "Please Give Me Something To Remember You By." And I'll bet it does.

When you've putted out and called your score, it's time to head for the clubhouse.

Our first stop will be in very close proximity to the golf shop. The reason is that your host or master scorekeeper will post your scores on the *handicap sheet*. If you have a handicap of 18 or less, the maximum score you will be charged for on any one hole—as far as the handicap is concerned—will be a *double bogie* (two over par). If however, as an example, you were playing at your 22, you will be allowed a maximum of four *triple bogies*. The rest—*double bogies, bogies, pars, birdies*—whatever you shot as a gross score, will be added for the score sheet. Every guest's score should be recorded on what's called an *away sheet*. The *away sheet* is where one notes the course rating, his adjusted gross score, his handicap I.D. number, his name, and the name of the course just played. You will appear thorough, detailed, and responsible if you have acquired your handicap I.D. number from your home pro. Lacking that, it would be smart of you to state you are in the process of getting your handicap I.D. number. All amateur golf is played using an official handicap. So it behooves everyone to see to it that his scores are recorded so that an established handicap can be assigned to you from the sanctioning golf association responsible for the geographic area in which you play. Many clubs are now doing this by computer.

There's one other little nuance you should know about at a private club. If you've taken a cart, it is presumed that your host will have charged it to his account. If you take a caddie, sometimes paid by cash, it's proper protocol, at the end of the round, to ask your host if you may pay your caddie at the rate he normally pays his caddie. Do not pay your caddie more than he pays his. More than likely, however, he'll say forget it, it's all taken care of. This one singular cash gesture, however, is on the approved list, as well as one other to be discussed in the next chapter.

The Final Locker Room Visit

Most golfers prefer to disrobe at their locker and head for the showers. It is not in keeping with the golf locker room atmosphere to walk about naked. So the idea is to secure a towel that can be wrapped around oneself en route to the showers.

It's likely that at the private club there will be a separate room for wash basins, hair grooming, and the like. If beauty potions are there, use what you will. Leave no tip. Place cloth towels in the cloth disposal. Paper towels in the paper disposal.

A change of sports shirt may be desirable at this point, or shirt, tie and jacket, if headed for the dining room. As you arrive at the locker room, hand your golf shoes to the head locker room attendant and ask him if he would prepare them for your departure.

While you're showering, your golf shoes will be cleaned and probably placed in a plastic carry bag that will fit into your shoe bag or case for departure. It's at this point you find the locker room attendant and, with quiet aplomb, palm him his tip, for shining not only your dress shoes, but your golf shoes. At the time of this writing, a five-dollar bill is pretty much a *minimum* standard. Thank him for the use of the locker and leave it unlocked. He will tend to it from there.

Don't worry about your golf bag. The Caddie Master, or someone similarly assigned, will have already taken your bag to the outgoing rack, the same rack where you deposited your clubs upon arrival. If you wish to confirm this, you may ask the locker room attendant, "Will my bag of clubs be placed in the out-rack for departure?"

The
Accounting
Room

You say it looks an awful lot like the Grill? You're quite right. It normally is one and the same. We will take a table with the other players, and the master scorekeeper of our group will figure out the financial responsibilities each has incurred during this "athletic" contest.

At least two of the other players will question his addition, subtraction, and general accuracy. If it's all new and confusing, sit and smile and let 'em wonder how smart you are. Everyone will eventually be told what he is collecting or what is owed. This is a cash transaction. No IOUs. No credit cards. No checks. Cash on the barrelhead.

It's also a great time to recount shots, usually with comments like, "I really only hit a couple of good ones today." And if I only had done this, and I only had done that. And if my aunt were endowed differently she would be my uncle. Other gadflies will drop by and ask various players how they did. They in turn will lament that it was a terrible day but surely tomorrow looms brighter. How did you hit it? "Frequently," will often be the answer. There'll probably be some nice compliments paid at this time too. "You sure did shinny up that tree great in order to retrieve that ball." "When you fell in the canyon, I just knew you'd be able to climb out." "You sure did cut that ol' indestructible ball, didn't you?" "Slidin' down that hill kinda stained your pants, didn't it?" "When your ball hit that tree, hey, hey, and it came right back atcha, boy you moved like a bandit!" And someone will probably say to you solicitously, "With a little bit more instruction, and experience, you hold forth great promise." That's a compliment.

But the most ultimate of compliments will be, "I enjoyed your company. I hope we can do it again." Ah ha! You've made a net impression! Done a good job establishing your image!

Drinks are normally now in order. The bar is open for some tall tales of funny incidents of previous rounds, great moments remembered, and good fellowship. The whole thing might be just building up to a gin game. If you fancy yourself adept at the paste cards, join in.

Here's a story I can contribute to "moments remembered."

It's a couple of observations about the great Walter Hagen, for whom I had the pleasure of caddying many, many summers ago.

First of all, at least in my own experience and contrary to myth, I never saw the man intoxicated. And that business of him always carrying a flask in his golf bag, I can assure you, from my experience, was pure hokum. Oh, he was flamboyant! And I do believe that he wanted to encourage his playboy image.

The first time I caddied for him, he was playing an exhibition. Since it was an exhibition match, he was not limited to fourteen clubs. He had three putters in his bag. We came to a hole where he had to sink an approximate four-foot putt. I am now convinced he could have knocked it square into the hole with a hoe handle. I handed him the putter he had been using. He strode elegantly upon the green in his golf knickers in front of an intense gallery, waggled the putter a time or two, came back over to me, and said in a rather loud voice, "No, Bailey. Wrong putter." And I handed him a second putter from his bag and he paced back onto the green again, waggled it a few times and came back to me and said in a loud voice, "Not this one, the other one!" He then went back onto the green and of course knocked the ball right into the center of the hole. The crowd applauded, and as he came back to me at his bag, I said, "I'm sorry, Mr. Hagen." And he said, in a stage whisper, "Hey, don't worry kid, we got to have a little fun with these folks." He was great theater.

The other memory that lingers is one that has much to do with the positive thinking philosophy that is expounded in every "how to" article or book we pick up today. In most golf instructional books, they say, "*Visualize* the shot you intend to make." The Haig *talked* to himself in a quiet voice before each shot, or almost every shot. This one instance stands out in my mind.

He had selected a brassie, now called a 2-wood, a club that is almost passe. As I handed him his club, he said softly to himself, "I hit it low between those two trees with a slight fade and it lands on that right hillside, rolling left into the fairway for perfect position." He didn't just think positively. He called an audible! And the footnote to the story is interesting. As he hit that shot, he miss-hit it, badly hooking it around both of the trees, but the ball did land approximately where he wanted it to land, in good fairway position. The crowd roared their approval. As he placed the club back into my hands, he said, "Only you and I will ever know the truth." This saying was a ritual, when he did miscalculate occasionally. But his audible "system" of preconditioning himself was standard. It was an experience each time I was with him. This story is in keeping with the nature of this book. We visualize our conduct before arriving on the golf scene.

Perhaps we even describe to ourselves the actions and attitudes we wish to portray. We clearly define the image we would most like to establish during our four-hour interview or observation time. It's a great way to set the stage for our own curtain call.

The
Departure

You've done your thing and hopefully you had an excellent lesson in the etiquette of golf. You've found a greater appreciation of golf; that it requires self-reliance, responsibility, integrity, and trust—many great image attributes. Was it worth it? As someone said, "Where else can you find this amount of humiliation, this amount of frustration, with this amount of self-challenge to conquer yourself and influence others?"

If you've visited a private club, drop your host a note of thanks. One of these days the pay-off will be handsome in its rewards of good fellowship and perhaps great opportunity. Irrespective of the score, you've taken a giant step forward in learning and minding your manners in golf. Make it the forerunner of many happy rounds to come.

It is not merely a sport, as Armon Alchian said in his article in *The Wall Street Journal*, golf "is an activity, a lifestyle, *a behavior* [my emphasis], a manifestation of the essential human spirit. Golf's ethics, principles, rules, and procedures are totally capitalistic." And as executive golfers, we understand what that's all about!

For now we come to the great moment of truth about your image. Image is what actually distinguishes you from all others. Facts only stitch the edge of the total tapestry that is a composite of all the impressions you've made. Human evaluation is not based on logic as many would suppose, but more on the emotional, impressionistic level. In short, your image is your reality, and you alone can shape the image that will bring you much happiness. May that include your great enjoyment of golf and its many benefits that so many thousands of us have found. That's what this book is all about.

"Your black shoes, sir, are ready for you,
complementing your black tie and tux."
But of course! Executive, all the way.

Glossary

Ace: A hole in one.

Approach: A stroke played to the putting green, or to the pin if possible.

Apron: Grass area immediately bordering the putting surface, generally mowed about halfway. Same as *fringe*.

Away: The ball farthest away from the hole when more than one golfer is playing. The golfer whose ball is away plays first.

Backspin: A reverse spin put on the ball to make it stop on the putting green.

Backswing: The backward portion of the swing starting from the ground.

Ball in play: A ball is in play as soon as the player has made a stroke on the teeing ground. It remains in play as his ball until holed out, except when it is out of bounds or lost.

Ball lost: A ball is lost if (A) it cannot be found within five minutes; (B) it is declared lost by the player without searching for five minutes.

Ball marker: A small coin or facsimile used to spot a ball's position on the putting green.

Beach: Any sand hazard on the golf course.

Birdie: One stroke under the designated par of a hole.

Bite: Backspin imparted to a ball.

Bogey: One stroke over the designated par of a hole.

Bunker: An area of bare ground, often a depression, which is usually covered with sand. It falls under the category of "hazard."

Caddie: A person who carries or handles a player's clubs during play and otherwise assists him.

Carry: Distance from the place where the ball is struck to the place where it first strikes the ground.

Chip shot: A short approach of low trajectory, usually from near the putting green.

Clubhouse: A building that houses such facilities as lockers, restaurant, bar, and card and meeting rooms.

Competitor: A fellow competitor is any player with whom the golfer plays.

Course: A golf course usually is 9 or 18 holes, each hole consisting of a tee, fairway, and putting green.

Course rating: The evaluation of the playing difficulty of a course compared with other rated courses.

Divot: Piece of turf cut out by a club head during a stroke.

Dog-leg: A bend in the fairway either to the right or to the left.

Double bogey: A score of 2 over par for a single hole.

Drive: To hit a ball from a tee.

Eagle: Two strokes under the designated par for a hole.

Fairway: The well-kept portion of terrain between the tee and putting green.

Flagstick: A moveable staff or pole placed in the hole on the green to show its location. Same as *flag* or *pin*.

Fore: An expression called out in warning to those in danger from the flight of the ball. Also, when said quietly like, "Fore, please," means you're moving, talking, or causing a distraction. Be still.

Gimme: A putt so short that it will most likely be conceded by an opponent.

Green fee: The fee paid for the privilege of playing on the golf course.

Handicap: The stroke or strokes a player may deduct from his gross, or actual, score.

Hole: A round receptacle in the green.

Hole in one: A hole made in one stroke.

Home pro: A professional who maintains his position at a golf club to teach, and plays only in local events.

Honor: The right or privilege of hitting first from the tee, which goes to the winner of the preceding hole or the last hole won.

In the leather: A term in friendly matches allowing (or giving) a putt that is quite short in distance from ball to cup.

Iron: Club with a metal head. From the number 2 through the wedge, the iron face becomes larger and more lofted.

Lateral hazard: Any water hazard running approximately parallel to the line of play.

Lie: The position in which the ball rests on the ground.

Match play: A golf competition played by holes—each hole is a separate contest—rather than total score. The team or player winning the greatest number of holes is the winner.

Medal Play: A competition decided by total, overall score, with every stroke counting. Same as *Stroke Play.*

Mulligan: A second shot, usually off the first tee, that is sometimes permitted in a casual social game, but never in a competition.

Out of bounds: The ground outside of the course, on which play is prohibited.

Par: The theoretical number of strokes a player should take to complete a hole.

Penalty stroke: A stroke added to a player's score for violation of rules.

PGA: Professional Golfers Association.

Pin: Same as *flagstick.*

Pro shop: A place to buy golf equipment; it is operated by the club professional.

Provisional ball: A ball played after the previous ball is thought to have been lost or out of bounds.

Putt: Stroking the ball toward the hole on the putting green.

Putter: Club used on the putting green.

Sand trap: A hazard containing sand.

Short game: The shots of pitching, chipping, and putting.

Snake: A very long, winding putt, as in, "I sank a snake."

Stroke: Any forward motion of the club head made with intent to hit and move the ball, successful or not.

Stroke hole: The hole on which a player applies a handicap stroke. The numerical order in which handicap strokes are allocated, are shown on the scorecard.

Summer rules: USGA playing rules of golf apply. You do not improve your lie. You play the ball exactly where it comes to rest.

Tee: A wood or plastic device on which the ball is placed for driving. Also the area from which the ball is driven on the first shot of each hole.

Up: The number of holes or strokes a player is ahead of his opponent.

USGA: United States Golf Association.

Whiff: To miss the ball completely.

Winter rules: The USGA recognizes no such rule in checking a "preferred lie" (meaning you move the ball to suit you). However, some *local* rules, and sometimes PGA rules, allow the player to "pick and clean," but *only* under the most adverse weather conditions, and then it must be posted as a temporary condition of play.

Index

About the Author

Bill Bailey is a business executive whose passion is the game of golf. For some forty-five years he's played the game in the United States and abroad. He's competitive, and carries a low handicap and a high regard for golf's influence in the business world.

Starting as a caddie, he preferred 75 cents a loop (eighteen holes) to hoeing dockweed or other chores on his parents' Ohio farm. Big moments in his youth included caddying for the great Walter Hagen and Patty Berg.

He captained his school's golf team, Regis, in Denver, played some amateur competitive golf on a national basis and then country club golf in Chicago, which he has played since. He's currently a member of twenty-three years' standing at La Jolla Country Club and a member of Signature Country Clubs, which is dedicated to multiple membership in a number of premier clubs throughout the world.

With a background in broadcast journalism, he was associated with both NBC and CBS for a number of years as a writer, producer, performer, and spokesperson. He is now Executive Vice President of Marketing for Signature Country Clubs International.

"I'm sure my deportment on the golf course has not always been exemplary. But I respect the game so much, I wish it were so. Perhaps the thoughts gathered in this little book will help guide some people away from the roughs that entrap the 'Bunglers of Golf Behavior.'"

Churchill
on Leadership

Executive Success in the Face of Adversity

Steven F. Hayward

U.S. $20.00
Can. $26.95
ISBN: 0-7615-0855-4
hardcover / 224 pages

"Perhaps the finest book on practical leadership ever written."
—Brian Tracy

In business as in government, success often depends on the strength of a single quality: leadership. Winston Churchill is universally recognized as one of the 20th century's great political leaders, and his words and example ring just as true in the world of commerce. Author Steven F. Hayward draws

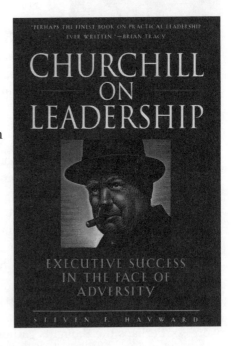

on Churchill's rich legacy to offer trenchant lessons in leadership for business people today. His book brings the titan of history to vibrant life as a wise, witty, and inspiring leader who ran Great Britain like a great corporation.

Visit us online at www.primapublishing.com

Blowing Smoke

Being a Compendium of Amusing Anecdotes,
Witty Ripostes, and Lengthy Literary Passages
on the Glories of the Cigar

Mary Foley and Kevin Foley

U.S. $13.00
Can. $17.95
ISBN: 0-7615-1098-2
hardcover / 96 pages

"If I can't smoke
in Heaven, I shall not
go there."
—Mark Twain

Collecting the words of
such famed cigar
aficionados as Mark
Twain, Winston
Churchill, H. G. Wells,
and Ernest Hemingway,
this exclusive selection
of amusing, anecdotal

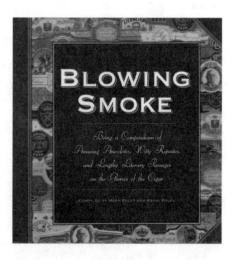

tobacco lore lights up the world of cigars, proving once and
for all that if you enjoy a fine stogie you're in good company.

Mary and Kevin Foley own the Cigar Locker, a retail store
in Granite Bay, California, where they frequently host cigar
evenings for their customers.

Visit us online at www.primapublishing.com

To Order Books

Please send me the following items:

Quantity	Title	Unit Price	Total
_____	**Churchill on Leadership**	$ 20.00	$ _____
_____	**Blowing Smoke**	$ 13.00	$ _____
_____	_____	$ _____	$ _____
_____	_____	$ _____	$ _____
_____	_____	$ _____	$ _____

*Shipping and Handling depend on Subtotal.

Subtotal	Shipping/Handling
$0.00–$14.99	$3.00
$15.00–$29.99	$4.00
$30.00–$49.99	$6.00
$50.00–$99.99	$10.00
$100.00–$199.99	$13.50
$200.00+	Call for Quote

Foreign and all Priority Request orders:
Call Order Entry department
for price quote at 916-632-4400

This chart represents the total retail price of books only (before applicable discounts are taken).

Subtotal $ _____
Deduct 10% when ordering 3-5 books $ _____
7.25% Sales Tax (CA only) $ _____
8.25% Sales Tax (TN only) $ _____
5.0% Sales Tax (MD and IN only) $ _____
7.0% G.S.T. Tax (Canada only) $ _____
Shipping and Handling* $ _____
Total Order $ _____

By Telephone: With MC or Visa, call 800-632-8676 or 916-632-4400. Mon–Fri, 8:30-4:30.

WWW: http://www.primapublishing.com

By Internet E-mail: sales@primapub.com

By Mail: Just fill out the information below and send with your remittance to:

**Prima Publishing
P.O. Box 1260BK
Rocklin, CA 95677**

My name is _____

I live at _____

City _____ State _____ ZIP _____

MC/Visa#_____ Exp. _____

Check/money order enclosed for $_____ Payable to Prima Publishing

Daytime telephone _____

Signature _____